Advance praise for *Badluck Way*

"In this unforgettable memoir, Bryce Andrews conjures the modern West with all its grit and conflict. At its core lies the old grudge between livestock protection and predator control. This fine memoir contains meticulous details of onerous ranch work—the unexpected violence of herding cows, the backbreak labor of building fence. Haunting and lyrical, this marvelous work belongs on everyone's bookshelf alongside other Western Classics."

—Craig Lesley, author of *Winterkill* and *The Sky Fisherman*

"One could find no better guide than Bryce Andrews for a journey along the shifting border between the wild and the tame; a daunting frontier filled with unsettling truths, blood, and beauty. His wonderfully crafted prose is lean, yet rich in the telling details of seasons spent on a Montana ranch overseeing a shaky coexistence between cattle and wolves. Andrews is a keen-eyed ecologist, a skilled ranch hand and, best of all, a self-examining student of life with a young man's inclination to push past fear and caution toward an embrace of risky, life-altering experience. In *Badluck Way,* Andrews shuns both cowboy romanticism and environmentalist sermonizing and illuminates the inescapable conflict between human economic imperatives and the compulsions of animal instinct. His book is a gripping tale of the West, raw and real."

—David Horsey, columnist and cartoonist for
the *Los Angeles Times*

"Bryce Andrews's *Badluck Way* is a powerful invocation of place and landscape narrated in a voice energetic, earnest, and wise. Year-round ranch work—tough, physical, and weathered—combined with a hard-earned regard and affection for animals—both livestock and wild creatures—thread together to renew our faith in the power of place, the value of work, and the ever-present need to interrogate our own lives and livelihoods."

—Phil Condon, author of *Montana Surround*
and *Nine Ten Again*

"*Badluck Way* addresses clearly, concisely, and eloquently a year when individual belief, faith, and philosophy are tested and tempered daily by the physical, communal, and political. On Montana's Sun Ranch, . . . grass, granite, and ice, wolves, elk, livestock, and humans coalesce to shape in sharp relief the vital and contentious issues facing our region and society. Andrews offers a remarkably rounded, informed, and yes, wise, perspective. *Badluck Way* is a powerful testament from a new writer with much to share."

—Robert Stubblefield, the University of Montana

BADLUCK
WAY

C.1

BADLUCK WAY

– A Year on the Ragged Edge of the West –

BRYCE ANDREWS

ATRIA BOOKS

New York   London   Toronto   Sydney   New Delhi

ATRIA BOOKS

A Division of Simon & Schuster, Inc.
1230 Avenue of the Americas
New York, NY 10020

Certain names and identifying characteristics have been changed, and certain events have been reordered and combined.

First Atria Books hardcover edition January 2014

ATRIA BOOKS and colophon are trademarks of Simon & Schuster, Inc.

For information about special discounts for bulk purchases, please contact Simon & Schuster Special Sales at 1-866-506-1949 or business@simonandschuster.com.

The Simon & Schuster Speakers Bureau can bring authors to your live event. For more information or to book an event contact the Simon & Schuster Speakers Bureau at 1-866-248-3049 or visit our website at www.simonspeakers.com.

Designed by Paul Dippolito
Map by Kendra McKlosky
Photographs by Bryce Andrews

Manufactured in the United States of America

10   9   8   7   6   5   4   3   2   1

Library of Congress Cataloging-in-Publication Data

Andrews, Bryce.
  Badluck Way : a year on the ragged edge of the West / Bryce Andrews.—
First Atria Books hardcover edition.
    pages cm
  1. Andrews, Bryce. 2. Wolves—Montana. 3. Human-wolf encounters—Montana. 4. Ranch life—Montana. 5. Ranchers—Montana —Biography. 6. Montana—Biography. 7. Montana—Description and travel. 8. Lee Metcalf Wilderness (Mont.)—Description and travel. 9. Madison River Valley (Wyo. and Mont.)—Description and travel. I. Title.
    F735.2.A53A3 2013
    978.6—dc23   2013011635

ISBN 978-1-4767-1083-9
ISBN 978-1-4767-1085-3 (ebook)

Contents

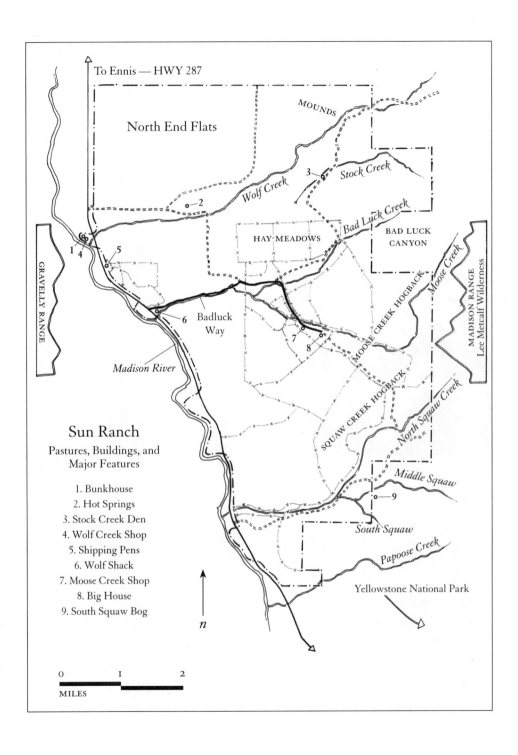

To Ennis — HWY 287

MOUNDS

North End Flats

Stock Creek

3

Wolf Creek

2

HAY MEADOWS

Bad Luck Creek

BAD LUCK
CANYON

Moose Creek

1 4

5

GRAVELLY RANGE

MADISON RANGE
Lee Metcalf Wilderness

MOOSE CREEK HOGBACK

6

Badluck
Way

7

8

Madison River

SQUAW CREEK HOGBACK

North Squaw Creek

Middle Squaw

9

Sun Ranch

Pastures, Buildings, and
Major Features

1. Bunkhouse
2. Hot Springs
3. Stock Creek Den
4. Wolf Creek Shop
5. Shipping Pens
6. Wolf Shack
7. Moose Creek Shop
8. Big House
9. South Squaw Bog

South Squaw

Papoose Creek

Yellowstone National Park

n

0   1   2

MILES

Prologue

When the sun dropped behind the highest ridge of the Gravelly Range, I sat on my front porch and watched daylight quit the Madison Valley. In April, at six thousand feet, night came quickly.

Once the big orb winked out of sight, the day's hard, pale light and meager heat poured across the western horizon in a torrent. Warm colors went first and fastest, balling up in an eddy of red, orange, and ocher before slipping from view. I imagined those hues flowing across the Gravellies to glint on the small-town storefronts of Twin Bridges and reflect in the slow oxbows of the Beaverhead River. I pictured them gaining speed as they fled westward through the Big Hole drainage and then skipping like stones across mountains, valley, mountains, and so on to the sea.

The other, colder colors drained more slowly from the sky, moving across the valley in procession, each rising above the towering bench behind the house and tracking west by degrees. Green came first, then every hue of blue. The last color in the train was fathomless, abyssal. It lingered, a deep, pelagic shade that rolled slowly through the world, enveloping everything and leaving full darkness in its wake. The crescent moon followed some distance behind it, like a tagalong kid brother.

I was alone in the cold, crystalline night, thirty miles from a town of any consequence, staring out across the seldom-traveled gravel track that we on the Sun Ranch called Badluck Way. The failing light made it easy to remember the land as it had looked in summer. In my mind's eye the hills glowed golden under a late-July sun. Tall, drying bunchgrass bent against the wind and fed the ranch's vast herds of cattle. Antelope scudded across the horizon like clouds before a storm, and half a dozen gin-clear creeks tumbled downhill between stands of green, close-set willows. Above it all, in the high country, wolves and other wild creatures made endless, inscrutable loops across the ridges and valleys.

The bustle and toil of life in August—long days on horseback and barbwire fence work—had raised a thick network of scabs and scars on my hands. Some of the scars remained, but they were the least of the high season's bloody relics. Staring into the darkness beyond Badluck Way, I returned to the moments that had demanded violence of me. Alone in the dark I threw old punches again and set my finger against the rifle's trigger once more.

After one year on the Sun Ranch, a year of work, sweat, and hard choices, I was thinking about leaving. Dwindling snowdrifts dotted the landscape, some sculpted by the wind, others the consequence of my winter plowing. These latter piles stretched out along the road for half a mile and stopped at the intersection with Highway 287. I strained to see beyond the highway, to the dense willows that grow along the Madison, but the night was too complete.

The high and faraway whine of a diesel engine spooling up from the south reached me, building in volume and complexity. In the perfect silence of the Madison, the sound of a tractor-trailer switching gears was audible from miles away.

The truck appeared suddenly, when it rounded a bend where

the highway swings wide around the river. Small amber lights outlined its cab and trailer. From a distance these resolved into simple
geometric shapes—a long rectangle in hot pursuit of a straining
right triangle. The truck roared past the turn for Badluck Way
without slowing down, then picked up speed until it hit the big
hill at Wolf Creek. It downshifted once, then again when the engine began to lag and groan.

Though he could not see it, the trucker was rising up from the
plain of the Madison, climbing the grade to the Cameron bench.
Through his left window, across the river, were the sheer basalt
cliffs of the Palisades. To his right was the ranch's North End. Beyond the little world of his headlights were seven square miles of
open grassland, fifteen hundred grazing elk, and the wolves that
kept them moving through the night.

When the truck topped the hill, I stood to go back into the
house. From a great distance in that vast, black landscape, the rig
looked as lonely as an ocean liner.

My house on Badluck Way was a log prefab, designed in the
shape of a wide H by an architect who never had intended to live in
it. He'd drawn cramped rooms, sparse light fixtures, and a drafty
brick fireplace that kept the place cold no matter how much wood
was burning. The house must have come in two pieces, because
the laundry room's floor plan was a mirror image of the kitchen's.

Living there, I had come to hate the crevices between the wall
logs. They gobbled incandescent light like candy and soaked up
most of the glow from the cabin's few small windows. A good log
wall can be a masterpiece. Neatly joined and thoroughly chinked,
it can stand against the elements for decades. A good wall is snug
and monolithic, a bulwark against the wild. My walls were sieves,

the logs sloppily joined and sealed piecemeal with brownish caulk. On clear days the rooms were flecked with glowing slivers of sunlight. During storms the wind hissed in. When summer gave way to the first real cold of fall, the logs disgorged an unsettling number and variety of spiders.

Despite its careful orientation on the open, sunny north bank of Moose Creek, the house was always dark and a bit cold inside. Walking through its door felt like going underground into a cave or den. Because of this we called it the Wolf Shack.

The front porch was a concrete slab between the wings of the house, kept sunless by an overhanging roof. An identical back porch was buried under a landslide of firewood, shed antlers, rusty leghold traps, and other detritus. In spring, when the world began to thaw and the weather allowed, I ate dinner out front. Deer, elk, or hamburger from town went onto the grill of my little Coleman barbecue. When the meat was ready, I ate leaning forward to catch the heat rising from the coals.

Most of the time I stayed comfortable on the porch, even when the temperature dropped below freezing, because the house blocked everything except a straight north wind. I watched stars emerge to fill the void above the Wolf Shack and thought back to the beginning of my time on the ranch.

– I –

ON THE SUN

Eastbound to the West

One way to say how I ended up on the Sun is that my life in Walla Walla, Washington, where I'd stacked basalt, poured concrete foundations, and waited for a girl to finish her last year of college, ended. The door slammed shut and I just kept moving, out of desperation more than anything else. I went home to Seattle, slept on the floor in a friend's house in Fremont, and knocked around miserably in bars. Then I joined up with another buddy, who lived on a sailboat that was thirty years old and twenty-eight feet long, and sailed that tub up to the San Juan Islands in a January storm. I was at the helm when the boom snapped in half and threw us broadside to the swells. As I fought the wheel and Bill cursed his rickety diesel inboard motor, I thought about how small the warmth of my body was and how endless the chill of water. I thought of how things thrown in the ocean sink down beyond the reach of the sun. Waves broke over the bow and it was raining so hard that I breathed through my nose to keep from choking. In spite of oilskins, rubber boots, a plastic hood, and neoprene gloves, I was soaked to the skin.

When the motor finally kicked over, Bill folded the sail into a packet no bigger than a bedsheet, and we limped against the storm back toward Port Townsend. Veils of rain hid the Olympic Peninsula, so it seemed the world was made of only water. I tasted the ocean. It flooded my eyes. I watched it rise into jagged topographies that passed like mountain ranges on the move. When we docked, I had to pry my hands from around the wheel. I stepped onto dry land and thought: Enough.

Getting lost was easy. One day I went down to the Amtrak station and slid out of Seattle on a pair of steel rails, traveling three unwashed days down the coast to San Diego, where I surfed poorly and did chores for my grandparents. My grandfather was on the mend from his first go-round with cancer. Though we couldn't walk the beach together, he was optimistic when he left me at the station.

I took trains that rattled across the Southwest: Phoenix, Tucson, San Antonio, and a hundred map dots in between. I got a hotel room in New Orleans for my twenty-third birthday, did what everyone does there, then ran north to get away. From D.C. and New York to Chicago, where clinker ice hissed against a concrete breakwater, I was quick and free. My feet had barely touched the ground since California. I bought a southbound ticket and one week later crossed into Juárez, Mexico, in the middle of the night.

It makes a difference when your money runs out, especially in Mexico. I ate tacos of dubious provenance, scraped through the twisting innards of the Copper Canyon, and hitchhiked up Baja in a propane delivery truck with no starter and no brakes. After crossing back into the States at Tijuana, I spent three days retching in my grandparents' bathroom, and went home to Seattle feeling as though I could handle just about anything. I looked for work, and the first good thing I found was a summer ranch job.

That's one way to explain how I got to the Sun.

Another way to say it is that, ever since I can remember, I've been obsessed with the West. I grew up in Seattle, the son of a professional photographer and an art director. My father started running the University of Washington's art museum when I was four and kept the job for twenty years. He must have had a touch of my own mania, because when I was seven he organized a show called *The Myth of the West*. While the curators installed it, I played with balls of wadded masking tape in front of Albert Bierstadt's light-soaked picture of Yellowstone Falls and practiced my quick draw facing Andy Warhol's duded-up *Double Elvis*.

Dad brought home crowds of artists from work to eat at our long kitchen table. I was six when Pat Zentz came to dinner and kept everyone up with stories until night gave way to morning. In Seattle's art scene, Pat was something different. He hailed from a ranch outside of Billings: a two-thousand-acre spread of dryland wheat, old homestead buildings, Black Angus cattle, grass, and sky where he built sculptures and worked like hell to keep from losing the land. One of these summers, Pat said, we should come out and see it.

Our first visit to the Zentz Ranch, when I was seven years old, lasted only a couple of days. We pulled spotted knapweed with Pat, his wife, Suzie, and their three boys and helped move a few cows on horseback. My mother photographed every skeletal cottonwood and disintegrating outbuilding she could find. On the last evening, we drove out to a high bluff that Pat called Martini Ridge and watched the sky grow dark above the Crazy Mountains. Emergent stars seemed closer than the horizon. When we left I pressed my face to a dusty backseat window and cried.

I came back the next summer—stayed longer, worked a little bit harder, got paid two bucks an hour. I learned to roll up rusty, ground-bound strands of barbwire. In the summers that followed, I built fence, fixed fence, moved cows, and learned how to catch and tack a horse. I drove a 1978 GMC High Sierra on tracks so rough my forehead smacked the steering wheel. When the work was done I lay faceup on the truck's roof looking into the deep blue bowl of the sky. Thunderstorms rose in the southwest, raged a short while, and then blew east to die in the Badlands. The smell of wet dirt followed.

Every summer until I turned eighteen, I returned to the Zentz Ranch to work for nothing, or next to nothing, finding recompense in the little calluses on my palms. Whenever I went home to the damp claustrophobia of Seattle, I would dream about big, dry, lonely country. I pictured it each time I bought a ticket to anywhere or filled up the gas tank on my truck.

After returning from Mexico, when I sat down in front of my parents' computer to look for a job, I could not put the idea of ranching from my mind. I found a job announcement on the Montana State University website. The first paragraph read:

The Sun Ranch is located on the edge of the Lee Metcalf Wilderness, in the upper Madison River Valley of southwestern Montana, about 30 miles south of Ennis. It encompasses approximately 25,000 acres of deeded land and grazing leases. The Ranch is committed to conservation and improving the health of the land for wildlife and livestock through progressive management.

The position was seasonal, a six-month gig beginning on the first of May. The job title was Assistant Grazing Technician/Livestock Manager. Of the nine traits listed as the "Successful Applicant's Qualities," six were unremarkable, couched in the narcotic jargon of human resources, but the last three were different. I read them slowly and more than once: "Common Sense, Adaptability, Gumption."

I did a little research and found that the Sun Ranch straddles one of the most important wildlife corridors in the Greater Yellowstone Ecosystem, providing habitat for grizzly bears, wolves, lynx, and wolverines. Elk herds numbering in the thousands move across it. The ranch was at the vanguard of a movement to rethink the way agriculture is practiced in the West. Large herds of yearling cattle grazed the ranch each summer. The movement of these heifers and steers across the landscape was carefully choreographed to complement, rather than hinder, the systems of the wild. Simply put, the idea was to integrate ranching into a functional, natural ecosystem.

The Madison Valley, and especially the south end of the Madison Valley, was my father's fishing heaven. He'd taken me to the river as a teenager, and we'd leapfrogged up the pocket water near Three Dollar Bridge. From my time on the Zentz place I knew a bit about the work described, the fencing and herding, anyway. I had gumption, or thought I did, so I called about the job and was hired.

On my last morning in Seattle, I packed the back of my truck with jeans and work shirts, a few cooking utensils, sheets, and food that would keep. I scuffed my cowboy boots against a curb so they wouldn't look brand-new and drove out of the city on wet streets, weaving through the morning rush.

Interstate 90 led toward the west slope of the Cascades. Ahead the clouds snugged down around Snoqualmie Pass and its attendant peaks like a gray skullcap. The forest pressed in from either side of the freeway—firs, cedars, and elephantine blackberry tangles. I charged up and over the pass. The walls of greenery blurred and then, somewhere after Cle Elum, disappeared.

I had practiced this departure many times, and as the irrigated fields and scrubland of eastern Washington unfurled in all directions, everything felt right. I was headed away from my youth and home, a place where the clouds spat water through a lush, evergreen canopy. Ahead, the horizon was wide and empty, and the sky a clear blue. I was eastbound toward the West, to become a ranch hand in the high country of Montana. I never even glanced at the rearview mirror.

I sped through wheat fields and orchards, slept in a ratty Coeur d'Alene motel, and crossed into Montana by way of the Idaho Panhandle. By four in the afternoon I was at the foot of the Norris hill.

If the Norris hill were someplace flatter than southwest Montana, it would be considered a mountain. Here, though, it's unremarkable, and probably wouldn't even merit a name if it weren't for the fact that Highway 287 climbs it to a saddle from which the whole Madison Valley is visible.

The view on the far side is distracting enough to cause a wreck. I pulled to the edge of the road to take it in. Two mountain ranges strike south from the hill, keeping roughly parallel to each other. In the foreground they are at least ten miles apart, but farther off the ranges bend inward, pinching off the valley like an hourglass waist. Though the valley is symmetrical in shape, the mountains that flank it could not be more different.

On the east side, the Madisons leap suddenly toward the blue sky. Sharp, sheer, and rocky, at first glance they seem to cant forward and overhang the valley slightly. My map named some of the peaks: Fan, Helmet, Sphinx, and Wedge. From the top of the Norris hill they look like a solid wall with broken shards of glass along the top.

The map also named a few of the Gravelly Range's westward mountains, but I could not match them to the landscape. While the Madisons form a line of glinting canine teeth, the Gravellies are a many-shouldered swelling of the earth. The fallen-down range humps up from the floodplain grass, rising into a maze of timbered ridges, flecked from bottom to top with open meadows of various sizes.

Rangeland begins where the foothills end, and the valley is wide enough to hold an ocean of grass. From atop the Norris hill, the landscape resolves into a series of descending benches, regular enough to look from a distance like a massive green-carpeted staircase connecting the mountains to the river.

The most striking part of it all was the Madison River, which reflected the afternoon sun and drew a golden line through the heart of the valley. Curving smoothly across the floodplain like a snake navigating stony ground, the river issues from the south and is flanked on either side by dark thickets of willow.

Traffic roared behind me, pulling my attention back to the early-season tourists and long-haul truckers topping the hill and accelerating down into the valley like roller-coaster cars. A little convoy of them dropped out of sight on a curve and reappeared on the far side of the town of Ennis. After Ennis, the highway crosses the Madison and veers south, running straight toward a little smudge in the grass called Cameron, population forty-nine.

According to my map, Cameron was fifteen miles from Ennis, and the Sun Ranch fifteen miles farther up the road. I stared south, following the twists and turns of the Madison River upstream to where the mountains squeezed in tight around it, trying to imagine how the ranch lay upon the land.

When I arrived on the Sun for the first time, Jeremy was standing in his front yard, waiting. For a long time I wondered how he had pulled that off, since I had given him the day, but not the time, of my arrival. No doubt he'd heard my truck clattering over the frontage road washboards or seen a dust trail rising. At any rate he was ready and I found him leaning against a low chain-link fence, looking like the boss in a broad straw hat and a sun-faded blue shirt.

"Glad you found it," he said, and shook my hand.

I thanked him for taking a chance on hiring me, and he laughed like I had told a good joke. Up close, Jeremy looked younger, almost baby-faced except for a light goatee and a pair of round photosensitive glasses. Under the high April sun, those glasses turned dark enough to hide his eyes entirely.

We talked in the yard, orbited by a pair of black border collies. Sometimes the dogs trotted up close to measure me with quick, inquisitive sniffs.

Jeremy took me on a walking tour of a cluster of buildings adjacent to his house. We looped through a machine shop, corrals, and a handful of old livestock sheds in slump-roofed subsidence. Because of the eponymous stream that ran behind these structures, the little settlement was known as Wolf Creek. In addition to the compound we were walking through, there was another clump of buildings in the dead center of the ranch, which included the owner's house, an old barn, the ranch office, and a sheet-metal building full of heavy equipment. Those constructions were scattered along a watercourse of their own, and were therefore called the Moose Creek buildings.

As we passed the various ranch trucks, parked in a neat line, Jeremy pointed at a massive white one-ton flatbed Ford.

"You'll share that one with James, when he gets here."

He left me at a low wooden bunkhouse, not far from the machine shop, with instructions to get settled in.

"See you in the morning," Jeremy said. "We leave at seven."

I had arrived.

The wolf came up Beaver Creek, quiet as fog. The Lee Metcalf Wilderness was new country to him, steeper and emptier than the high plateaus of Northern Yellowstone. He walked at night through the leftovers of hunting camps—smelled the places where men cooked and shat and gutted their quarry. He killed deer in the little meadows below Blue Danube Lake and cracked their long bones for marrow. Other wolves had already staked their claims to the land—he heard them howling in the night and kept his distance. In late fall, when the first real snow fell and the elk herds made their harrowing climb across the ten-thousand-foot-high saddle of Expedition Pass, he followed.

Coming down from Expedition through the pink granite cliffs that form a rampart between the Madison and Gallatin valleys, he was a long way from home. Below him, gathered in a rocky embrace, Finger Lake was rimed with a thin sheet of ice. He trotted around it, heading downhill through the thick timber along Moose Creek.

Wolves inhabit a landscape humans can never know. Their forest is different from the one we walk through—more intelligible, bursting at the seams with information. Because of the ample signs to lead him on, the wolf never doubted his direction as he followed the twists and turns of Moose Creek: elk turds strewn around like dark hailstones, little trees rubbed bare by rutting bulls, and, amid an unbroken procession of scents, the occasional scatter of rib cage and leg bones.

He trotted out of the trees, and onto the rocky spine of the Moose Creek hogback. From that perch he saw the Sun Ranch sprawling toward the Madison River. To the north, beyond the aspen groves of Wolf Creek, vast flats stretched off to the horizon. The nearest house was miles below him, dark and shuttered against the impending snap of winter. Just across the creek from the house, hundreds of steers flecked the flat grass expanse of the hay meadows.

The wolf turned south, away from the low country and the livestock. Crossing the enormous, triangular face of a huge foothill called the Pyramid, he dropped into Squaw Creek's labyrinth of fens and dark timber. He found it full of game and largely empty of wolves. He stayed.

The Lie of the Land

*O*n my first morning in the bunkhouse, I woke up shivering and listened to the harsh squalling of magpies. Through a little window, past trim boards cracked and shrunken by age and exposure, a handful of stars still pocked the predawn sky. I lay motionless as they faded into the daylight. An insistent, hissing wind slipped through gaps in the window casing. The Madison wind is pitiless. It is a sandblasting, constant presence, meant for howling around the eaves of broken shacks and the scattered bones of winter-killed cattle. Passing cold and dry across my skin, it reminded me how far I was from Seattle.

Jeremy and I went to fetch the horses. We piled into the ranch's flatbed Ford and drove north on the highway toward a neighboring ranch where the herd had wintered. As we climbed the first grade, the truck growled and shuddered against the weight of the trailer, and Jeremy pointed out landmarks: the road that followed Wolf Creek toward the mountains; various locked gates that provided access from the highway; the principal peaks and drainages; the old, wind-shredded homestead buildings that dotted the flats; and finally, the ranch's northern boundary.

The Sun Ranch horses had wintered with around fifty others, and the whole bunch was waiting in a dilapidated set of corrals. They milled together, blending into swirls of color and blowing steam into the morning cold.

Jeremy grabbed a bundle of halters from the trailer's tack compartment and handed all but one of them to me. Then the two of us walked into the corral. The horses pressed away, jostling each other to stay out of reach. As the herd reshuffled itself, Jeremy pointed out a horse that had stepped into view.

"That sorrel gelding," he said, "is Shooter."

The horse pricked up its ears as Jeremy took a step toward it. He moved another pace and the gelding shied away, melting back into the herd. Jeremy pressed on, moving slowly through the equine crowd, keeping his eyes on the sorrel and reacting to its movements with little corrections to his course. Quickly, almost magically, he sorted it off from its fellows. He reached out slowly to the horse's nose, face, and neck, slipped on the halter, tied it, and led Shooter out of the pen.

After tying Shooter to the trailer, Jeremy came back, grabbed a halter, and caught another horse—a tall bay gelding with a roman nose—with the same calm efficiency.

"This is Billy," he said as he passed me on the way out. "Billy's mine."

Jeremy caught two more horses. He walked right up to a dark-brown gelding named Skip. A fat mare named Tina took a couple of tries to corner, but followed willingly enough once the halter was on.

I had two halters left in my hand, and Jeremy took one of them. He pointed to a small paint horse, more white than brown, in the corral's far corner.

"Catch that TJ horse," Jeremy said. "He'll be one of yours."

TJ watched suspiciously as I crossed the corral. I mimicked Jeremy, moving slowly and carefully through the rest of the herd, adjusting my path as TJ stepped one way or the other. TJ stayed calm, even when I tripped over a pile of horseshit and staggered to the side. I stretched out a hand, touched the cold velvet of his nose, and slipped the halter on him.

"Nice," Jeremy said. "Now here's where it usually gets interesting."

The last horse on our list, Spook, was a paint like TJ, but the similarities ended there. TJ was calm, almost sleepy at the end of my halter rope. Spook, on the other hand, was the poster child for nervous energy. Standing a full head taller than the horses around him, Spook was covered in blotches of white and brown over a background of jet black. The overall effect was complex and foreboding, like thunderheads before a summer storm.

Jeremy took a step toward Spook, who tracked him with both ears. When Jeremy made another move, Spook took a deep breath and blew it out. One more step was enough to trip the trigger, and Spook made a beeline for the far corner of the pen, scattering the rest of the horses as he went. As Spook bolted, his tail flared behind him, midnight black with a single white stripe along its length, as though marked by lightning.

Spook took refuge in the far corner of the pen, and Jeremy followed him calmly. Each time Jeremy began to close in, the horse blew up, ran away, and hid in the herd. The practiced way that horse and man conducted the pursuit seemed familiar to both of them.

It took the better part of half an hour to catch Spook, who panted hard as Jeremy finally got the halter on. We led him out of the corral and tied him to the trailer with the others.

We wormed all six horses. I held their halters while Jeremy squirted a noxious cream down each of their throats in turn. None of them liked it. Spook reared and lifted me up off the ground. Tina tried to bite off Jeremy's fingers. Afterward we loaded them in a trailer and headed back to the Sun.

We didn't stay long at Wolf Creek, because Jeremy wanted to "leg up" the horses by riding them to the barn and pastures where they would spend the rest of the summer. He pointed out a saddle that would fit me, handed over TJ's lead rope, and turned his attention to getting Billy ready to ride.

I saddled TJ carefully, working hard to bend the stiff, dry

leather of cinch, latigo, and breast collar. After I'd mounted up and made a couple of laps around the shop, we headed out across the ranch. Jeremy rode first, with Shooter, Tina, and Spook in tow. I followed him, ponying Skip behind me. We crossed the highway, passed the ranch's sprawling corrals, and angled uphill on a trail through the short green grass.

As we rode, I wondered why Jeremy had chosen that day to catch the horses. We had no urgent need for them, since the summer cattle herd wouldn't be arriving for another few weeks and we could have been doing a number of more pressing tasks on the ranch. Jeremy was quiet until we crested a hill and left the highway behind. Then he reined in Billy and let me draw even with him.

As we rode together through what seemed like an endless sea of grass, Jeremy talked about the ranch and its history. He started with cows but gravitated to the subject of wolves, beginning with their reintroduction to Yellowstone National Park in 1995 and their subsequent colonization of adjacent valleys, like the Madison. Livestock depredations had followed in the tracks of the dispersing wolves, and the resulting debate had spread like wildfire through the discourse and politics of southwest Montana.

Working on the Sun Ranch put us right in the eye of the storm. Our pack, the Wedge Pack, was composed of wolves that had come across the Madison Range from Yellowstone. According to a state biologist, it amounted to nine adults, plus an unknown number of pups.

The Wedge Pack, like most others, was a family unit cen-

tered on a single breeding pair. Aerial surveys had reported that
two consecutive litters of pups had been successfully raised in the
foothills and steep valleys behind the Sun. Beyond that, it was
hard to say anything conclusive about the makeup of the pack,
since the wolves were in a constant state of flux: Alpha males and
females died or were deposed. Diseases like mange and distem-
per ripped through the population. With each new season, sons
and daughters of the pack grew into themselves and departed for
new territory.

Jeremy pointed uphill across the green expanse toward a deep,
sheer cleft in the Madison Range.

"They've been staying up in Bad Luck Creek."

The ranch had been lucky last year. The wolves had stuck to
killing elk, and the cattle had come home fat at the end of the
summer. This amounted to a very good thing, given the ranch's
emphasis on peaceful coexistence with wildlife. But Jeremy worried about the coming months. The pack had more mouths to feed
this year, and over the winter they had become increasingly bra-
zen and less terrified of human sight and scent. Jeremy had seen
some wolf kills; the pack could tear apart an elk before it had a
chance to die.

Jeremy got quiet then and rode in silence, taking my measure.
From time to time he glanced sideways to look, I imagined, at the
way I reined and spurred my horse. I sat up straight and did my
best to ride well.

I kept glancing up at the place where the wolves were. Bad
Luck Canyon stood out in the low gold light of afternoon, form-
ing a dark V in the mountains. The canyon held its shadow while

the rest of the world caught fire. It looked as though a piece of the panorama had been sliced away, and nothing put in its place to hide the blackness underneath.

• • •

In the days that followed our first ride, I learned that Jeremy ran a tight ship. He made up systems for organizing the necessities of life and was unique in diligently and unfailingly following his own rules. He was a labeler of drawers, and if one said "drill bits," you could bet there would be drill bits in it—all of them, and in good order.

He'd designed a bolt room on the ranch, a space the size of a walk-in closet lined on all sides with cubbyholes full of hardware. There were carriage bolts, lag bolts, lock washers, and nylon nuts. Most things were available in a staggering variety of sizes and at least two threads, and everything stayed in its proper place. When I came to the bolt room in desperate need of a specific piece of hardware, I usually found it advertised by a handwritten sign with particulars like: "3/8 carriage bolt—coarse."

Soft-spoken and almost always calm, Jeremy assigned me hard, complicated jobs, and explained them patiently. He taught me to move cattle without speaking much, by working the angles and applying gentle pressure to stragglers. He showed me how to run a backhoe, demonstrating the way bucket and hoe could move like extensions of my arms.

Because of his expertise and meticulous preparation, most of what we did went like clockwork. On just a few occasions, when the gate blew shut, a fence gave, or somebody failed to turn the herd, the harder side of Jeremy emerged: the features of his face clenched tight, and he cussed under his breath and charged top speed toward the problem, not stopping until he'd fixed it.

Jeremy moved fast. We had a Polaris Ranger on the ranch, a four-wheeler on steroids with a centrifugal clutch and two forward gears, low and high. The gears were marked "L" and "H" on the shifter, and I imagined that a third, secret gear above them, called "J," was used only by Jeremy in response to the minor emergencies that occur on a ranch.

It happened regularly enough: pausing a moment from work, I would watch the Ranger rocket down the gravel road, a speck throwing a dust trail big enough to see from space. Jeremy would quit the road at some open gate and go clanking across a pasture, mowing down sagebrush and catching air off badger holes. As the noise got fainter I would wonder what had gone wrong.

In the evenings Jeremy played bluegrass and folk songs on the guitar. He read Wendell Berry's essays, listened to *Democracy Now!* on satellite radio, and planned the following day's work. I believed that, behind his lighted windows, he was constantly teaching himself to build, fix, and run things, a theory corroborated by our daily work.

For my first two weeks, I checked and fixed barbwire fence. Under Jeremy's direction I pounded in staples and spliced wire where winter drifts, elk, or cattle had torn it apart. At the end of the day I went home exhausted, cooked a simple dinner, slept dreamless, and began again in the morning.

One Friday, I woke early and met Jeremy in the cold dawn. We climbed into his truck and drove south on the highway for a mile or so. Near Moose Creek, we turned off the pavement through a post-and-lintel gateway with a picture of the ranch's rising-sun brand and a sign bragging up the Sun's participation in something called the Undaunted Stewardship program. The road was gravel, but well maintained, and the addresses on a small clump of mailboxes identified it as Badluck Way. Off to the south, two log houses sat at the base of an enormous hill. Jeremy pointed at the smaller of the two.

"That's the Wolf Shack," he said. "The other one's called the Gatehouse."

Badluck Way was the ranch's major thoroughfare, since it began at the highway and ended at a cluster of buildings that included the owner's house, ranch office, equipment shop, and barn. It was worth my while, Jeremy said, to learn it like the back of my hand and get comfortable with driving it in all kinds of weather.

Badluck Way was actually a new moniker for the road—the result of a recent push by the post office and police dispatcher to name every significant track in the valley. A letter had been sent to Roger, the ranch's owner, asking whether he'd like to give the road a name, or simply stand aside and let the county assign it a number. To his credit, Roger decided to go the creative route.

"The road does come pretty close to Bad Luck Creek," Jeremy said, "but mostly I think he chose Badluck Way because it sounded good."

As we drove uphill along Moose Creek, I learned that the ranch occupied an irregular wedge of property between the sharp pinnacles of the mountains on one side and the parallel ribbons of the Madison River and Highway 287 on the other. This uneven Nevada could be divided, geographically speaking, into two distinct and contrasting hemispheres. The north half of the Sun Ranch was flat, massive, and open—a nearly endless expanse of waving grass that extended right up to the base of the mountains. Fences on the North End followed the section lines of an old survey, which gave it a reassuring, rectilinear predictability.

Not so on the South End. There the ranch tapered to a point and the land heaved up like wastepaper crumpled by a giant hand. The South End was full of steep ridges and twisted valleys, a chaotic, disorienting place. Crossing through meant hard traveling in the best of conditions. A bad winter storm could leave it impenetrable.

For the most part the ranch got wilder with elevation, which increased as you headed east from the river toward the mountains. The Moose Creek canyon, which was relatively low and close to the western edge of the property, was an exception. It began just a half mile from Highway 287, where Moose Creek and Badluck Way bunched together to enter a deep crease in the land. The slopes on either bank of the creek steepened to forty-five degrees. On the side where the road ran, a south-facing slope grew ryegrass and mullein. Across the creek, the north side bristled with an amphitheater of the oldest trees on the property. From the highway, the Moose Creek canyon's notch looked like an enormous gun sight pointed at the Madison Range.

Most of the canyon was too steep for cattle, and hunting had been prohibited there since Roger had driven up during hunting season, heard someone shooting at an elk, and decided he had almost taken a bullet. That happened years before I arrived on the ranch, and the intervening time had turned the canyon into an overgrown, mostly untracked wilderness.

The canyon worked as a funnel, gathering animals—elk, deer, antelope, and moose—from the higher benches of the ranch and channeling them downhill toward the Madison River. In winter, when higher trails drifted shut with snow, the population became especially dense. The wolves knew this, and could often be seen running the canyon during the dark and icy months.

Jeremy showed me elk paths worn into the hills and pointed out places where they crossed the road. The truck labored up a steep grade, shook as it passed over the last washboards of the canyon, and then emerged into full sunlight. The view was staggering. Straight ahead of us, Moose Creek wound through a broad swath of willows, looped around the base of a hill, and then struck straight east toward where the Madison Range jutted into a light-blue sky. Jeremy pointed out the Pyramid, a grassy, vertiginous triangle on the scale of Giza that formed the divide between the drainages of Moose and Squaw Creeks. Topping out at nine thousand feet, the Pyramid fell to eight thousand and then blended seamlessly into the low, broad hump of the Squaw Creek hogback.

Jeremy talked his way across the skyline from north to south, showing me the different gorges that gave birth to Wolf, Stock, Bad Luck, Moose, and Squaw Creeks. Flowing from the mountains toward the river, those five creeks bisected the ranch. If the Madison Range was the ranch's prime meridian, the streams were its preeminent lines of latitude. After Jeremy had pointed out the many dirt tracks that departed at intervals from Badluck Way, we descended a little hill to a small cluster of buildings, where he brought the truck to a stop in front of a sheet-metal shop.

Inside, the machines waited in good order. A fire truck occupied the only heated bay. Farther down, partially hidden in the windowless dark, were a road grader and a John Deere backhoe. Next to a collection of smaller machines, a plasticized map of the ranch hung on the wall. Jeremy unpinned it and handed it over. After showing me how to start one of the ATVs, a yellow Honda Foreman, he cut me loose to spend the rest of the day getting to know the Sun.

———•———

I rode the ATV out into the morning, bracing myself against the stream of cold air. The Foreman was a strong machine, a 500. I revved through the gears, watching the speedometer climb through twenty, thirty, and forty as I followed Badluck Way downhill. I turned right onto a smaller gravel track that struck off to the north and ran across level ground for a while before arriving at the brink of a steep descent.

I pulled out the map to get my bearings. Directly ahead, the road cruised across the Stock Creek plain, crossed a rickety bridge over Wolf Creek, and then struck out into a featureless zone of seven square miles called the North End Flats. Beyond that, the road met the ranch's northern boundary fence, cut eastward through an area labeled with the single, cryptic word "Mounds," and then looped back south along the base of the mountains, past Stock and Bad Luck Creeks.

I folded the map and sped away. Melting snowdrifts crossed the road at intervals, and I cut the spring's first tracks through them, scattering slush and mud as I roared onto the Flats. The endless sky was blue, and everywhere grass was rising from the dead. All of it augured a bright future.

The Foreman loved level ground and carried me across the Flats so fast I nearly missed seeing the ruins that sat perhaps a half mile from the road. Out there in the bunchgrass, a handful of slumping wooden shacks dotted the landscape. I shut off the engine and started toward them, but although I walked for a long time, the buildings never grew in size. The ATV, however, dwindled to a speck, nearly disappearing into the imperceptible topography of the Flats. Alarmed, I turned and hurried back to the Foreman, kicked it over, sped north, and didn't stop until I hit the boundary fence.

Riding east, things got interesting in a hurry as I buzzed toward the base of the mountains and into the Mounds, a tight clump of hills left over from the last spasms of glaciation. After miles of unsettling, severe expanse, the Mounds came as a welcome relief. With the gentle, rolling aspect of a golf course, the Mounds were a world unto themselves. In a landscape of exposure, they held you close. They grew the best grass on the ranch and the animals knew it. I stopped and walked awhile in the Mounds—found a little antler there, mouse-chewed and grayed by years.

Beyond the Mounds, the going turned rough and the ruts got so deep that I couldn't take my eyes off the ground. Because of this, Bad Luck Canyon sneaked up on me. One moment I was traveling alongside the reassuring face of a mountain and the next the canyon gaped open, a great, foreboding maw, close on my left-hand side.

Exploring that dark place had been my first thought when

Jeremy turned me loose for the day, and I had intended to hike at least a little ways up Bad Luck Creek. But there, at the mouth of the canyon, an old fear percolated up and tightened my throat. I let the Foreman idle and stared upstream to where the water disappeared between sharply angled walls of timber.

————•◦•————

In the summer three years ago, before I knew about the Sun Ranch, I had filled a backpack and walked up a switchback trail into the Lee Metcalf Wilderness. I carried too much: a hatchet, sandals, four pairs of socks, a change of pants, a novel, a cell phone, a notebook, toiletries, a two-man tent, and a GPS unit with bewildering functions. I was fresh off the highway from Seattle and the thought of bears nearly paralyzed me.

As I climbed up the east side of the Madison Range, ascending along Beaver Creek until the trees thinned and the trail wandered across patches of loose talus, I marveled at the sheer-sided valleys, shouted nonsense into the clear air, and waited for echoes. I strained beneath the weight of my rookie's pack and stopped often to pant and drink water.

After just a few uphill miles, I reached Blue Danube Lake. Because of my load and inexperience, I was exhausted. It seemed I had come to a place removed in not just space but time. Pink granite cliffs ringed the tarn on three sides. Mosquitoes rose in droves from the water and bunched thick around my face and hands. The only sign of human trespass was a handful of rusty tin cans marked with the names of companies long since foundered and dissolved.

I pitched my tent and sat beside it while the daylight waned, feeling lucky to have found my way into another, older world. Thunderheads rose in dark masses and slid like a lid across the day. First there was wind, then rain, and then lightning from a pitch-black sky.

The alpine bowl collected more than water—it magnified the noise and light of the storm. I did not sleep but lay on my thin foam pad, eyes straight up, as bolts struck all around the semicircle of peaks, bright as camera flashes. They dislodged hunks of stone that thundered close about the tent and splashed into the lake. The storm went on through the night, ending just before dawn broke, around five in the morning.

A single thought possessed me as I struck camp: Get out. I had planned to stay another day or two in the high country, to visit other lakes, but the night and storm changed everything. I was afraid, not just of bears but the possibility that these wild mountains might swallow me. It was no secret that they could—bones were everywhere.

The route had seemed clear enough on my map: circle around Blue Danube, clamber up to a saddle between two cliffs, bushwhack a mile to a small, unnamed lake, take a Forest Service trail four miles down Squaw Creek, and then follow a public easement across the Sun Ranch to the Madison River and Highway 287.

I might have made it, if not for the mosquitoes and biting flies. They came on with dawn and gave me no rest for hours. In combination with the leftovers of midnight terror, they drove me on when I should have stopped to read map, country, and compass. I did not eat. I hardly drank. Soon I was lost without a trail, plunging downhill along a spring, pushing through high willow thickets with both hands.

Hours and miles passed. Grunts and crashing noises issued from the willows, and at one panicked moment I uncapped my bear spray and pointed it futilely at a wall of close-set sticks. But nothing emerged and it was late afternoon when I struck the highway at Quake Lake, ten miles and ninety degrees of the compass away from the spot I was aiming for. I stood at the edge of the road, looked up at the mountains, and shivered. I told myself that I would not go back.

Standing next to the shadows of Bad Luck Canyon, the familiar fear rushed into me, the terror of feeling like prey in the mountains. I fled from it again, bouncing the Foreman south through Moose Creek and along the base of the Pyramid. Ahead of me, to the south, the ranch's property lines pinched down between the sheer cliffs of Hilgard Peak and the curling line of the river. The map showed a tangle of ridges, timber, and contorted streams, labeled with the words "Squaw Creek."

Snow lay deep in the road and kept me from venturing far into the South End that day. I dreaded getting my machine stuck. Instead, I shut off the engine, climbed to the top of a ridge, and looked out across the land.

Just as Jeremy had told me, the north and south halves of the Sun Ranch bore little resemblance to each other. North of Moose Creek, the land was defined by scale, order, and exposure. Views were sweeping up there, the fences followed survey lines, and crossing the landscape was mostly straightforward. In places, the North End Flats seemed limited only by the curvature of the earth. From the Flats, the Madison Range, though always visible, looked far away.

But to the south, beyond the open meadows that flanked Moose Creek, the topography bent into a great, chaotic knot. Ridges swept down from the mountains at strange angles, and the three forks of Squaw Creek veered crazily back and forth to negotiate them. The low places were choked with thick, dark timber. Even from a distance it looked like an easy place to get lost.

The wolf was not the first of his kind to stake a claim in Squaw Creek, below the sheer rocks of Hilgard Peak. Others, not long gone, had left their mark on the landscape. As he blundered into the places where they had killed elk and prowled through the mossy wreckage of skeletons, he discovered the best trails from one ridge to another and paused at scent trees that still held the last whiffs of stale urine. In time he found and cautiously entered the old dens. Nothing waited for him inside.

He tried to make sense of it, picking at the smells and leftover sign the way all canids do. A good cattle dog also knows the difference between fresh and stale wolf piss. He'll hackle up when faced with the new stuff, sometimes even growl or tuck his tail and press against the side of your leg. But old sign gives him pause. He knows it's not a threat, but pays attention anyhow. He sniffs it carefully, takes his time walking around, and eventually marks a tree or gatepost in a manner that somehow seems both assertive and deferential. From the way he acts, it is no great stretch to suppose that he's thinking hard about what came before him.

The wolf trotted along the steep ridge between the Middle and North Forks of Squaw Creek, with the high, hard peaks of the Lee Metcalf Wilderness spreading out south and east. In October, aspen trees would have been burning sunlight yellow in all the places where live water flows or springs rise close to the surface. The wolf would have been fat, full to bursting with offal and meat from some hapless mule deer. He would have followed the only good trail, the one that snakes between boulders, dipping often into the timber on the north side. The trail is the best route for everything that moves through Squaw Creek. Elk use it to gain elevation before they hit the rocky shins of Hilgard Peak. Grizzlies come in the early summer to flip boulders and swill down the grubs underneath. Because it is the easiest way through a tough piece of country, with a sweeping view of the open, grassy parks between the forks of the creek, ranch hands use it to check cattle.

The wolf trotted up that well-worn trail. He visited and refreshed the trees he used for marking territory. He watched, as everyone does from up there, the progress of cloud shadows across the sage and grass in the valley below. He stopped at a spot where something had scratched up a pile of fresh dirt. One whiff, and he knew he was no longer alone.

Rolling Rocks

W hen James's white crew-cab, long-box Chevy pulled into Wolf Creek, I thought that I had never seen a truck so thoroughly full. The cab was packed to the dome light and the box was piled high with tack, tools, plastic toys, and a bewildering array of camouflage camping gear. Behind the truck, a rusty bumper-pull trailer rattled and clanked with the noise of the impatient horses inside. The whole outfit rolled to a dusty stop outside Jeremy's house, and a big, redheaded guy in a flat-brimmed cowboy hat climbed down from the driver's seat.

I had come to the Sun Ranch in a little Toyota Tacoma with a small stock of gear. James had brought everything he could lift. After we shook hands, I helped him unearth an entire household from the truck bed and carry the bigger stuff inside the single-wide trailer that sat at the base of a hill across from my bunkhouse. Over the next half hour, we moved furniture, appliances, food, saddles, musical instruments, a good-sized TV, framed photos, and a queen-sized headboard, plus a half dozen pistols and at least that many rifles. James unloaded three horses from the trailer and turned them out to graze in the little pasture behind my house. Our last task was to unpack a doghouse and four panels of chain-link fence. We set the doghouse down near the corner of the trailer house and stood the panels up around it. As we worked, James told me that his herding dogs were en route, driving with his wife and kids from their home in Preston, Idaho.

———•———

James's world revolved around ranch work; his wife, Kendra; and his two young children. Beyond that, his favorite things were guns, hunting, old-time cowpoke yodeling, and trashy pop music. He had an open, easygoing charm and was a devout enough Mormon to abstain from beer, coffee, and swearing, three vices that he replaced with hard work and an endless stream of sugar. At home he was never without a big cup of Gatorade, and at the height of summer he went through an Otter Pops craze so intense it made my teeth hurt just to watch him. James gave me a copy of *The Book*. I might have read it if I weren't so stubborn, because I quickly grew to look up to him like an older brother.

Although we were both summer hands on the Sun and got paid about the same amount of money, James had far more experience. Almost through the Range Science program down at Utah State, with more than a few summers of ranch work under his belt, James was better than I was at every aspect of our work, and faster, too. When fixing fence together, we started at a gate and worked in opposite directions. I always tried to beat him to the halfway point, but never did. Panting, bleeding from a half dozen cuts, and stretching wire like a maniac, I would look up to see James's battered cowboy hat, red goatee, and broad shoulders pop over a ridge. Once in sight, he fairly whizzed down the line, stopping hardly long enough to see the breaks, let alone fix anything. His forearms stayed unscathed, as if the barbs were scared of them.

When the work was done, James took his time heading back to the shop. If there were cattle around he would suggest we ride through, "to settle them." Otherwise he devised some long way home that took us up into the foothills, past an old homestead or to some spot where he thought we might find elk antlers.

Once we were fixing a fence on the Forest Service allotment, a ragged one that snaked along a ridge and then shot straight up the face of a mountain. It ended where the slope got too steep for cattle. About halfway up the ridge, the fence met a public trail at right angles. When Jeremy had given us our marching orders, he'd mentioned that hikers and hunters often cut the wires, even though he had built a gate for them to use. Between that and the fact that a couple hundred head of elk had been crossing the ridge every dusk and dawn for six months, Jeremy figured that the fence would take us all day.

"After that," he said, "you're done."

We flew up that fence like dogs on a scent. The prospect of an afternoon off was that rare in early summer. Despite the fact that the whole stretch was uphill and torn to shit, I trotted from one break to the next, driving each new staple into the weathered posts with four hard swings of my fencing pliers.

The idea was to finish, turn around, and go home to take it easy, but at the top we were both gripped by a strange euphoria. Neither of us had ever fixed a fence that just plain ended. All the others turned corner after corner and put you right back at the start.

This was different. We stood uphill of the drift fence's end, feeling as though we had climbed beyond our ken. A sweeping view of the Madison River and the Gravelly Range unfolded to the west. Above it, the sky was pure blue. To the east was the steep-sided valley that held Squaw Creek, shaped by long-gone glacial ice into a broad-bottomed U. The slope around us was tattooed with the overlapping heart shapes of elk tracks and studded with dozens of roundish stones.

I slipped on a little boulder, knocking it loose. We watched the rock bound down the face of the mountain, leaping higher than a man's head, until it disappeared with a satisfying crash in a thicket of aspen. James climbed over to a basketball-sized stone and rocked it forward with his foot until gravity took over. The stone raced downhill, leaping higher and higher as though it wanted to fly. When it hit an old, gray pine, the snag shattered into half a dozen pieces. The game had begun.

We rolled rocks for an hour, dislodging every available boulder, competing for distance and to see who could flatten the biggest tree. It took both of our efforts to move some of the real Goliaths, and those huge stones cut wide swaths through the forest.

The whole business was as destructive as it was unnecessary. We smashed a lot of tree trunks, and couldn't have explained why we did it at the time. But now, at a little remove, I remember the thud and clatter of falling stone and the simple joy of watching trajectories unfold. As we chose our favorite rocks and sent them crashing through the woods, it seemed like our lives were consequential. For a few brief minutes, we were more than two specks on the steep shinbone of a mountain. We were shaping the wilderness, if only by punching holes. The land was stunning, enormous, and so empty that we didn't have to yell warnings to people down below. And for a handful of ecstatic moments, it all felt like our dominion.

When the best stones were gone, we looked across the valley. The smell of sap drifted up from dozens of ruined trees. We sat on the ground among little craters and looked out across the ranch, naming its seeps, bumps, and saddles. As if reciting a prayer, James listed off the common and scientific names of the plants that grew around our boots: yarrow—*Achillea millefolium;* big sage—*Artemisia tridentata;* bluebunch wheatgrass—*Agropyron spicatum;* and lupine—*Lupinus argenteus.*

Staring out across the folds and timber of Squaw Creek, we let our thoughts drift to the wolves. Sign of them abounded, though neither of us had yet seen one in the flesh. Holding out a clenched, massive fist for scale, James described a set of tracks he had found on a muddy stream bank just a few hundred yards above our houses. The pugmarks had looked exceptionally fresh, and their location meant that the wolves were traveling the lower pastures of the ranch. Though I was excited about the possibility of seeing the pack, James didn't like the situation. They were too close for comfort—his kids spent their days playing in the yard.

"I'll tell you one thing for sure," he said. "If that wolf comes around our place, he won't last long."

I never doubted that James or Jeremy would shoot a wolf if the opportunity arose. We talked of the pack often, and of the risks we would run when it came time to drive our herds higher into the mountains. In short order I learned that, to my role models, the killing of a wolf was no occasion for soul-searching. Instead it was a job that, though difficult and dangerous, sometimes had to be done.

When a person works long enough on a ranch, he comes to suspect that most of the living things that walk or grow on the hills and pastures are either with or against him. Smart cow dogs, calm horses, fertile heifers, and thick stands of wheatgrass are on a rancher's side. Noxious weeds and stock-killing predators stand decidedly against him.

James, in particular, had taken this lesson to heart. He told me once that he considered his animals to be part of his family, and felt an obligation to keep them from harm. That duty extended to the livestock, and as we worked together, I came to comprehend the depth of his loyalty to our herds.

James and Jeremy understood ranching as the art of protecting one's chosen creatures in a brutal world. Though sometimes this meant spilling blood, more often it demanded perfect attention and a depth of care—as with new calves and tender, growing shoots—that seemed at odds with their callused hands.

I must have been counted among the good animals, because James and Jeremy were always generous with me. They lent me essential things, gave good advice, and helped me take root in the Sun Ranch's hard soil.

Not long after James arrived on the ranch, I had finally gotten settled in the bunkhouse, a long, low, retrofitted shed that sat like an afterthought behind the other buildings at Wolf Creek. With its wonky floors and pair of rough barn doors that served as one wall of the kitchen, the bunkhouse leaked heat like a sieve. Through the crack between the doors, I could see the single-wide that James and his family called home.

One evening a ruckus started under the floor when I sat down to dinner. A series of thuds escalated into a screeching match and culminated in an unbearable smell that could mean only skunks. Gasping and coughing, I stumbled out of the kitchen and into the twilight, walked across to James's trailer, and told him the story.

"Well," said James, "I guess you better shoot it."

He handed me an old twelve gauge and a couple of shells. I walked to the most likely corner of the bunkhouse and waited. Standing in the dying light, I looked carefully at the shotgun, a cheap single-shot covered with little rust pits. I snapped it open and clicked it shut as the night thickened around me. No skunks showed, but I kept the gun for a few days.

My coats were all made for Seattle, so I borrowed a frayed Carhartt from Jeremy. The canvas was almost worn out, and in some places had rubbed away to reveal insulation, but I wore it every morning until summer got going.

I had no rope, so James dug out an old lariat and showed me how to coil and throw it. Jeremy pulled a saddle from the dusty innards of the barn, bought a new cinch for it, and helped me adjust the stirrups to the length of my legs. I found a pair of chaps that almost fit me in a corner of the tack room and begged a crumpled straw hat off my dad when he stopped by to visit and fish the Madison. Even with a ream of paper stuffed in the brim, that hat refused to stay with me on a loping horse. When I looked in the mirror, the overall effect was less than impressive.

I made $1,650 a month at the Sun Ranch and spent most of it on food, drink, and gear. In short order I returned James's old twelve gauge and bought myself a pump-action. I replaced the ill-fitting chaps with a pair of custom chinks from the leather shop on the edge of Ennis, switched from Levi's 501s to Wranglers, bought a palm-leaf hat with a leather band, and came home from a weekend trip to Sheridan, Wyoming, carrying a thirty-five-foot lariat with a left-handed twist. The transformation was slow and subtle enough to go unnoticed until one day I rode my horse past a window and saw a cowboy reflected.

I made a remark to that effect the next time I saw Jeremy, and he grimaced.

"I don't like the word *cowboy,* except as a verb," he said. I wished I hadn't mentioned it.

* * *

I drove into Ennis on a Saturday night for dinner and ended up drinking at the Silver Dollar, a knock-around place with elk racks on the walls, video poker machines in the corner, and a handful of regulars getting serious at the bar. I ordered a Pendleton whiskey and sat close enough to listen.

At first, the conversation revolved around the arrival of the year's first big batch of tourists. Spring was thawing into summer, and fly fishermen across the world knew it. Each morning brought a new wave of them through town, and their vehicles dotted the twists and turns of the Madison. From the hills above, those cars looked like beer cans strewn along the river.

From time to time I caught snatches of more interesting conversation. Down at the far end of the line of drinkers, a thick, spectacled man in a grubby black Stetson was holding forth to a handful of listeners. I strained to hear him over the low din of other talk. The man, I gathered, was a longtime resident of Virginia City, a defunct mining town just over the pass from Ennis, near the Ruby River.

"Guy named Bud Otis," the man began, "his daddy built VC up in the thirties. I shot his dog. Woke up to the sound of sheep crashing into the walls of my house, grabbed my rifle, and wounded the goddamn thing. It went up to Bud's and died."

One of the man's listeners mumbled something, but I couldn't catch it.

" 'Course I went to see him," the Stetson guy replied. "I wasn't no chickenshit. I went and he challenged me to a knife fight. Butcher knives, he said. Bud was in a wheelchair and I declined to fight him. Later, he was waiting for me outside the Bale of Hay with a pistol. Wanted to shoot me. I jumped behind an ore car and got to yelling: 'Bud, you couldn't hit shit, you son of a bitch!' Best part of it is I was right in front of my mother-in-law's place. She was some kind of witch—a real bitch, I mean. I kept hollering for Bud to shoot, hoping he'd break one of her windows and she'd be on him like stink on shit, but finally Jim came out and told Bud to put his gun away and go home."

I sipped my drink, trying to decide how much of what I heard was bull, until one of the two guys nearest to me, a nail keg of a man, leaned in toward the other, dropped his voice, and asked:

"What did you see up Squaw Creek?"

The questioner's close-cropped gray hair was tucked into a baseball cap with a flame paint job on the brim.

"Plenty of sign," the second man said, his face all but hidden by a wide-brimmed felt hat and a thick brown beard. "There's shit all over the place and a bunch of new kills. Couple bears, one sow griz with grown cubs, but mostly wolves. Lots of wolves."

"Goddamn," said the bearded man's buddy. "Could be a hell of a summer."

"Hard to say. We did all right with the first bunch for a couple years, even after the pack got big."

"Sure," said the man with the flaming hat. "But how did it end?"

He put on a canvas jacket, excused himself, and walked into the night. The bearded man went on drinking at the bar, and on an impulse I went over and sat down next to him. I explained that

I had just started working on the Sun and wanted to learn everything I could about the area, the animals, and the ranch.

The man, Steve, had worked in the backcountry of the Madison for years, doing wildlife surveys and packing into the Lee Metcalf as a Forest Service contractor. He knew the Sun Ranch well, and as I peppered him with questions, he patiently told me what he knew about its history.

The Sun Ranch hadn't always been its present eighteen thousand acres. Beginning in the early twentieth century, it was stitched together from individual homesteads. By the 1930s, the ranch's remoteness, elevation, and breathtaking panoramas had turned it from a patchwork of smallholdings into a rich man's paradise. The Sun grew aggressively through the early twentieth century, gobbling up smaller spreads as it expanded. Before World War II, it was called the Rising Sun Ranch, a name that started to chafe after news of Pearl Harbor reached the valley and was abandoned before the war's end. The Rising Sun lived on, however, in the Sun Ranch's brand—a four-spoked half circle that looks like dawn in open country.

After the name changed, the boundaries began to shift as well. The ranch passed through the hands of a series of absentee landowners, expanding or shrinking a bit each time the deeds changed hands.

Across the river from the Sun Ranch's western border, a sizable chunk of land came up for sale. The property, once known as the Granite Mountain Stock Ranch, stretched from the Madison River to the timbered slopes of the Gravelly Range. Like the Sun, it was empty and wild.

The new buyer looked east, saw the late-afternoon clouds catch fire above the scarps of the Madisons, and watched great herds of cattle and elk move back and forth from the low pastures to the mountains. Recognizing that those things and the cowboy dream that underlay them could be sold, he renamed his spread the Sun West Ranch, drew up plats, and started advertising homesites. New facilities took shape quickly, including a massive horse barn, an indoor riding arena, and a private shooting range. A few dozen millionaires bought into the idea, foundations got poured, and the deal was sealed.

Though it, too, circulated through various echelons of the ultrarich, the Sun Ranch stayed empty and undeveloped, perhaps because it exerts an immediate, irresistible power over people who come to know it. The Sun Ranch is wild, pure, and untrammeled to a degree that is rare anywhere else. Carving it up would be like scribbling on the *Mona Lisa*.

"Nobody would develop it," I said.

"I don't know about that," Steve replied. "The bottom part of Squaw Creek is platted out for a subdivision. All the paperwork is done, but I don't think Roger would ever act on it."

In any case, the Sun Ranch had managed to stay intact over the years. As time passed and other parts of the valley were gridded out into twenty-acre plots, its vastness and location became ever more important. For wild animals, the Sun provided a much-needed refuge from the constant noise and pressure of man. Pronghorn antelope migrated through by the hundreds, and elk lived and died by the winter forage they found on the ranch's North End. Moose fared better on the Sun than anywhere else in the valley. At the top of the ecosystem, grizzlies and wolves grew fat, multiplied, and dispersed to new territories. In the parlance of biologists, the Sun Ranch was known as a "population source."

Walking down Main Street in the dark, I thought about two notable artifacts on the ranch left over from the action hero's tenure: a pair of log cabins from a movie shoot below the beginning of Bad Luck Canyon and a stone hot tub in the absolute middle of nowhere.

Made of stacked logs and set on stone foundations, the cabins are meant to look scenic and old, and they do. By now they have outlasted any interest in the film for which they were built.

I spent one night in the bigger of the two cabins when we had a herd of cow-calf pairs bedded down nearby and the wolves were prowling through. Mice kept me awake, but other than that, the cabins were unused. They'd sat through storms and turned gray, settling on their foundations until no trace of Hollywood remained. Given a few more decades of freeze, thaw, and wind, they would be indistinguishable from half a dozen other homestead shacks on the place.

The action hero's other legacy was a bit more useful. Before selling the ranch, he'd engaged the services of a renowned mason from Ennis. The contractor had hauled load after load of cobbles from a nearby creek and cemented them into a massive tub. Pink, green, and black, the stones were smooth to the touch and as big around as beach balls. The tub was a low cylinder, fourteen feet across and four deep—beautiful craftsmanship.

The water came out of the ground fifty feet away and collected in a crystal-clear scalding pool, the kind for which Yellowstone Park is famous. Strange, thick algae grew in the pond, and a steel pipe ran downhill from it to curl over the tub's east wall like a kitchen faucet. The pipe gushed hot water day and night.

At night, the stars above the tub were so beautiful that I wore

"In other words," he said, "it's extremely goddamn important."

By way of example, he told me how the first wolves to recolonize the Madison Valley after their 1995 reintroduction to Yellowstone had made a home on the Sun. They had come out of the park in search of a place with the right mix of prey, topography, and emptiness. Out of the immense landscape that surrounds the Madison River, they took up residence on the ranch, dug in, and began to multiply. The pack grew until it numbered somewhere around ten wolves. In time, a biologist from the department of Fish, Wildlife & Parks managed to dart and collar a member of the pack. From then on, something was known of the movements of the Taylor Peak Pack, which they named after a mountain not far to the north.

With telemetry units clicking, ranch hands and biologists could follow the wolves across the drainages of the ranch and record the number, timing, and position of elk kills. A few of the elk got collars, too, as part of a study designed to explore predator-prey interactions.

Things went well for a while. The radio collars recorded the Taylor Peak wolves' perfect adaptation to a harsh environment. Researchers listened in as the pack followed elk into the uppermost reaches of the Lee Metcalf Wilderness. Occasionally a lucky intern or graduate student got to watch the ancient, evolutionary game of the hunt play out, the elk pounding across the open southern faces of the hills, the wolves in hot pursuit, straining their lungs and legs to keep up. Not far below, livestock continued to graze peacefully on the ranch.

Then came 2003: As spring gave way to summer, the elk headed for higher ground. Instead of tagging along, the wolves stuck around and crossed the river to Sun West, where hundreds of sheep were being used to control noxious weeds. One bloody night left a handful of carcasses on the ground. The wolves found sheep killing so easy they could not give it up. By the end of summer, the Taylor Peak Pack's alpha female had been gunned down from a USDA helicopter, and her offspring had been scattered throughout the valley.

The following summer was worse. Cows died. Wolves died. Attrition. In the end, the whole pack was wiped out with shotgun blasts from a helicopter door.

After the extermination of the Taylors, the south end of the Madison stayed quiet for a year. When wolves began turning up again, people assumed that they had come across from Yellowstone. The Wedge Pack, Steve concluded, was a wholly different group of animals, and he hoped that they would come to a different end.

"Enough about the wolves," Steve said. "I'll tell you about the movie star who owned that place before Roger."

He started in, suggesting that I take what I heard with a grain of salt, since most of the stories had been passed around the bars and kitchen tables of Ennis a few times. It was hard to say what had really gone on out there, since few people had access to the ranch until Roger bought it. Still, in a valley like the Madison, stories got around.

The previous owner had made his fortune as the leading man in a series of early-nineties shoot-'em-up movies. The way Steve heard it, this action hero liked to fly his buddies in and turn them loose on the ranch. One of the regulars was especially fond of hot-rodding across the Sun in a lifted, tinted black Suburban—a

monster truck. The guy rumbled across the North End, bouncing in and out of the old ditches and over the cairns built by Depression-era shepherds. He packed a handgun big enough to match the truck and blazed away at whatever caught his eye.

The legal targets would have been bunchgrass, cow pies, cans rusted and new, occasional shed antlers, rabbits, old homesteads, and coyotes. He preferred coyotes. With the radio blasting, the window wide open, and the AC blowing, he spent the long evenings of summer chasing them across the Flats. His favorite method of dispatch was to pull up alongside and shoot from the driver's seat.

At least once he missed his mark and found the pistol empty. The exhausted coyote edged ahead. The driver looked across the heaving line of his quarry's backbone and mashed the gas pedal until the V-8 screamed.

Steve stopped there, paused, and then shrugged.

"Could be a bunch of bullshit, but that's what I heard."

He paid his tab and shook my hand. Pulling on a dirty oilcloth coat, Steve nodded to the other guys drinking at the bar and took his leave.

As I waited to settle up with the bartender, I listened to more talk from the regulars. Down at the far end of the bar, the man in the black Stetson was still going strong about his days as a deputy sheriff. When I stood to go he was midway through a story about some notorious Virginia City woman who ended up handcuffed to the side-view mirror of his cruiser.

"I put it in gear and drove right down the street," he said. "She jumped on the hood and broke off both windshield wipers.

"Goddamn." He chuckled. "She had a sense of humor."

out my neck looking up. I spent hours soaking, swimming circles, and listening to the faraway drone of airliners. I traced dark skylines with my eyes: first the slump-shouldered hills of the Gravelly Range, then the toothy peaks of the Madisons. A tiny pinprick glow from a talc mine fifteen miles away was the only man-made light.

When I used the tub I thought of its builder rolling and hefting the stones, and then concentrating on the meticulous task of cementing them together. He must have worked for weeks, maybe months, to set the boulders as precisely as jewels. I compared those labors to my own job of fencing, herding, doctoring cows, and setting out salt, and came away impressed.

———•·•———

The clerk at the Ennis grocery store asked me where I worked. When I told her, she said she knew a lot about Roger. They hadn't ever talked, she admitted, but she held forth on how much he loved the wolves and his future plans for the Sun Ranch. She called him a "greenie" and lowered her voice to tell me about the time he refused to let a couple of local guys hunt moose on the ranch.

Her story had the ring of gossip to it, and I soon learned that Roger was a favorite and frequent subject of conversation in the Madison Valley. The particulars of his daily life constituted minor news, and some of his antics at the various picnics, auctions, and gatherings that punctuate the rural calendar were front-page material.

In the eyes of the valley's old-guard ranching community, Roger was a consummate outsider. A Stanford grad and Bay Area native, Roger had made his hundreds of millions in the original

Silicon Valley software boom, ending up filthy rich at a fairly young age.

Roger was a well-intentioned conservationist and an avid fly fisherman. Like so many who embrace that avocation, he loved Montana passionately. In this way, his story and mine are similar: We came to Montana first as fishermen, caught big rainbows and hook-jawed browns in the late afternoons of August and watched them break the surface of the Madison. As they slung drops of clear, cold water into the low sunlight, we promised to return. We huddled through winters in dense, coastal cities and laid plans to find our way back to the mountains, the river, and the endless Big Sky.

There our paths diverged. I had come to the Madison in a little truck, with just enough for gas and groceries in my checking account. Roger had bought the best eighteen thousand acres of the valley for twenty-seven million dollars. With the deed in hand, he announced his commitment to conservation ranching and his intention to open a high-end lodge catering to "eco-tourists" on an adjoining property.

In a place where ranching was a way of life and *California* a dirty word, this made waves. At fire department meetings and around kitchen tables, people began to talk. Locals wondered if they would be able to hunt elk on the Sun Ranch and speculated about whether Roger might kick the cattle off for good. They suspected that he might be too busy hugging trees and French-kissing grizzly bears to be neighborly.

Roger did his best to nip the worst rumors in the bud and assuage the more reasonable fears. He stuck with the cows, even embraced them as a tool for fertilizing soil, controlling weeds, and reinvigorating bunchgrass communities that thrived on periodic disturbance. He gave generously to local charities—the Rocky Mountain Elk Foundation, the Madison Valley Ranchlands Group, and others. He sponsored events.

I watched a video of Roger speaking at an annual summer party for the Ranchlands Group's Weed Committee, which was held under a huge, open-sided white plastic tent along the river. Men on horseback flagged down the arriving cars and pickup trucks and parked them in equal rows in the high grass. After some brief remarks by the weed coordinator about the importance of continuing the valley-wide extermination of hound's-tongue, spotted knapweed, Canada thistle, toadflax, and other noxious plants, Roger took the stage.

No real explanation was given for his presence up there, but it seemed like everyone in the audience knew who he was and that he had in all likelihood paid for the party. Roger greeted the crowd. Then, to break the ice, he said the following:

"I told my friends in California I was coming to a weed party in Montana. 'Whoa!' they said. 'What kind of people are you hanging out with up there?'"

He paused, and a good chunk of the audience laughed.

"One thing at a time, I told them. One thing at a time."

The few chuckles that followed seemed nervous, forced. Roger paused and then launched into a lengthy description of the strides that had been made to control weeds on the Sun Ranch, the importance of working together, and his commitment to the health and future of the Madison Valley.

Yet, in spite of himself, Roger was controversial. When he put half of the ranch in a conservation easement with the Nature Conservancy, neighbors took notice. When he leased irrigation water to Trout Unlimited, drying up a hundred acres of hay, it caused a stir. Roger was an emissary from a largely foreign world that promised nothing certain except for sweeping change. As such, he created curiosity and friction in equal measure.

Even on the ranch, we hired hands talked about Roger more than we talked with him. In addition to the Sun, Roger owned a telecommunications company up in Bozeman and Papoose Creek Lodge, a five-star cluster of log buildings just off Highway 287. Though the lodge was immediately adjacent to the southwest corner of the ranch, it functioned in a separate world.

Papoose Creek had its own herd of horses for trail rides, a chef, a wrangler, an outfitter, several managerial and administrative levels, and an ever-changing rabble of domestics, groundskeepers, and kitchen staff. It employed a handful of fishing guides in summer and an equal number of hunting guides in fall. Most of them lived in a cluster of cabins between the highway and the river—a cramped, noisy spot called the Madison Bend. You could get a beer down there at a place called the Grizzly Bar. The Griz catered mostly to fishermen, which meant that the food was good, if a little expensive.

The lodge staff earned their wages by making life easy for wealthy dudes, and I had a hard time forgiving them for it. They worked a good deal less than the ranch crew, and probably made more money when you counted all the tips.

I seldom went to Papoose Creek, and the lodge staff rarely made it up onto the high, sere benches of the ranch. We lived apart with one major exception: each Wednesday, the lodge held a barbecue on the bank of lower Squaw Creek. All the guests piled into a wagon drawn by two matched Percherons, and the whole ensemble made the arduous journey of a half mile across a lush pasture where the lodge grazed their horses. Arriving at their destination, the guests were treated to a dinner of mammoth proportions.

Every week, work permitting, one or two members of the ranch crew were allowed to join the festivities. The idea, as I understood it, was to lend a bit of authenticity to the proceedings, mingle with the guests and answer any questions about the ranch that might arise. In other words: show up covered in dirt, with blistered hands and worn-out jeans, and act like a cowboy. In exchange for this, we got to eat slow-cooked ribs; barbecued chicken; roasted vegetables; multiple pasta, potato, and green salads; fresh bread; and the finest baked beans I've had before or since. Those beans held a special power over me. I fantasized about them at dinnertime on days other than Wednesday, comparing them in my mind to whatever leftover pasta or lonesome steak I was eating.

Roger didn't get his money's worth from me at those dinners. I spent most of my time with my mouth full, and the balance of it drinking beer with the pretty girls hired to help the chef, serve the food, hold the horses, and do the other hundred chores necessary to live ostentatiously in the wilderness. Still, I usually got to tell a few stories and take a couple of questions before the guests were ready to head home. After helping see them off, I walked to the spot where I had hidden my ranch truck, waited until I was sure they couldn't hear the engine fire, and then headed down the bumpy road toward home.

Beyond the ranch and lodge, Roger had property in a handful

of states and seemed to make a fairly regular circuit of his homes and holdings, with far-flung vacation trips thrown in to break the monotony. We kept the Big House warm for him, but he didn't visit much in early spring.

From Jeremy and others I heard that Roger spent huge sums of money every year at the auctions run by local conservation groups. Relics from his spending sprees were scattered across the ranch. One weekend afternoon I set out from the bunkhouse, walked through a culvert that goes under Highway 287, and poked my head into the old calving barn that sat next to the creek. Inside I found a dry-docked flotilla: inflatables for running rough water, a ski boat with a massive outboard, and a pair of aluminum drift boats that looked brand-new except for a coating of dust and bird shit. While poking through another old shed, this one behind Jeremy's house, I found a wooden crate that held an unused birch canoe.

After seeing that pristine collection, I didn't expect Roger to pull up to the bunkhouse in a muddy Subaru. I didn't picture him small of stature with a boyish grin, dressed in faded jeans and a pair of black over-the-glasses shades that hid his face from nose to forehead. But that was Roger.

He stepped out of the car, walked over to me, and stuck out his hand.

"You must be Bryce."

I was a little disappointed. I thought the owner of a twenty-seven-million-dollar ranch would at least wear a gold watch or fancy shoes. Instead, Roger looked like a fisherman, like my father on vacation, right down to the quick-dry shirt with a fly shop's name stitched across the breast pocket.

Roger asked about the accommodations and how I liked my work so far. We talked for a couple of minutes before he excused himself and drove off to his house for a conference call. "Stop by anytime I'm up there," he said.

Roger was courteous, kind to his employees, and curious about the workings of the ranch, but he was always pressed for time. He skipped from one commitment to the next like a stone across water—there and gone in an instant, leaving ripples behind.

Two wolves wandered separately through the foothills of the Madison Range. The land was sliding into winter, and deep snow had driven hundreds of elk down from the peaks. At night the elk drifted out of the hills to graze on the flat, lush pastures of the ranch. They squealed and chirped to each other in the dark. Though both wolves began to haunt the edges of big, milling herds, the two of them did not get together right away—such things are usually complicated. They orbited each other, sniffing at tracks and keeping a safe distance. They courted across half a dozen drainages and bounced howls off the bottom of the moon.

Even as he made sense of the new presence, the wolf continued to learn his country. Down on the South End, he found his way into and out of the Squaw Creek bog, a trail-less rat's nest of broken timber, moss, and deep sinkholes. He discovered the overgrown logging road that cuts partway through the bog and used it thereafter as a shortcut. On Moose Creek, he patterned elk, learning which trails they used to cross through the foothills and where they chose to graze at night. Up Bad Luck Creek he found a perfect little defile, almost a box canyon, with live water and a well-worn game trail running through the bottom. He returned to it often until the elk grew wary and the canyon floor was littered with bones.

As he traveled, the wolf grew bolder. He learned the contours of the lower ranch and left a line of palm-sized tracks across the road when fresh snow covered the gravel of Badluck Way. From a lofty remove, he watched a bewildering variety of machines growl across the landscape. He saw men come and go from the shop and barn, and watched as they rode horseback to gather cattle. He kept a wary distance.

In time, he found ways to become invisible, honing this skill to a razor's edge on the North End, where every misstep sent deer and antelope scattering to the far horizon. That broad plain was a wild ungulate's dream, a place where the deck was stacked in favor of the prey and solidly against the predator. Nearly every spot out there had a commanding view, and the ground was perfect for running. When large, vigilant herds grazed the Flats, it took a stroke of luck for wolves to get anywhere near them.

The wolf still managed to eat. He followed the gentle, almost indistinguishable swales that wind across the Flats. He covered open ground at night and ambushed deer when they came down to the creek for water. When those tactics failed, he hunted smaller game—voles, rabbits, and anything else he could get his teeth around. From time to time, as he walked a creek or paused on his way through one of many high parks in his territory, he caught whiffs of the female's scent.

Near dusk and on the hunt, the wolf climbed to the top of a steep ridge, peered into the basin below, and caught sight of her standing at an old kill. She looked up from the bones and scattered tufts of belly hair, saw him standing near the tree line, and froze. She did not run. They drew together in the sage, sniffing at each other with tails held high. They came to an understanding and became something more than isolate wanderers out of Yellowstone.

Things moved quickly after that. They traveled together, hunted in tandem, and grew better at bringing down elk. In a little grove of timber on the south side of Stock Creek—a spot with a commanding view of the North End Flats and the strange, jumbled group of hills called the Mounds—they found an old den dug in beneath a massive pine.

A handful of wolfless years had left the den in ruins. Freeze and thaw, coupled with the creeping progress of roots, had conspired to bring the roof down in a heap of loose clods. The wolves dug in turns, pitching the dirt backward through their hind legs and into the light of day. In time, they excavated a gently sloping tunnel extending five or six feet into the hill. Though big enough for a thin man to wriggle into, the tunnel was tight, and its halfway point was marked by a sharp turn made to negotiate the pine's main taproot. A few feet beyond, the tunnel opened up into the den proper—a low, roundish chamber studded all over with roots.

When the tunnel was sufficiently clear and the den tidied to their satisfaction, the wolves turned their attention back to the everyday work of survival. They struck south to prowl the steep, wild terrain of Bad Luck Canyon. They returned often, however, to tinker with their hole. After each new bout of labor, sprays of fresh dirt marked the base of the pine.

The Line

*T*he Sun Ranch didn't winter any cattle. From October through May the
range belonged to wildlife, especially elk that
trailed across Expedition Pass each fall from
Yellowstone Park, walking nose to rump
across scree slopes and down the little trails
that filigree the high country. When it started
to snow the elk came en masse, numbering

two or three thousand. Huge herds gathered on the windswept flats of the ranch's North End. Smaller bunches cruised the steeper, forested drainages to the south.

Elk are beautiful and strange. Larger and darker than deer, they smell like wilderness. Not long into my tenure on the ranch, I went out walking after the workday was over. Just south of Bad Luck Creek, I topped a little hill and saw a herd of five hundred spread across the grass and sage like a painter's spill. The edge of the herd was close, no more than two hundred yards away. I quickly dropped on one knee behind a good-sized bush, but it was too late. The head of a near cow shot up. Her nose pointed skyward and her ears twisted dexterously. She gave a loud, guttural cough and the whole herd was off, moving like a stream of water across the pasture. They came to a fence, balled up for a moment, and then spilled across it. The wires groaned and snapped with their passing.

A big herd of elk is a striking thing, enough to make a person stop and stare. It is also hell on fences. Because of this, the bulk of my first month on the Sun Ranch was spent fencing. I had a leavening of other jobs, but they were utterly eclipsed by an endless procession of posts and wire splices.

The history of the Sun, like that of most other big spreads, is recorded in the type and position of its fences. The ranch was eighteen thousand deeded acres, plus a substantial Forest Service grazing allotment, and it contained every kind of cow barrier imaginable. There were barbwire fences and high-tensile ones, suspension fences and let-down fences, rail fences, jacklegs, old fences, and new ones.

My days were tangled up in wire and dried elk shit, which

rolled underneath my boots. In certain places, like the little grassy bowl we called Snowball, the elk crossed habitually. Up there the wires were shredded, more splice than space in between. I spent hours patching them back together—kneeling on the ground, twisting wire, grunting, sweating, and bleeding from forearm scratches. Months later, during hunting season, I remembered the precise routes that elk use to move across the ranch.

After a few days of splicing barbwire, nothing sounds quite so good as working on a let-down fence. Most of ours were a three-wire electric design, with the wires attached to stout wooden posts by plastic pin-lock insulators. In the fall, after the cattle were shipped off, someone would walk the line and pull all the pins. The wires fell to the ground and lay there all winter, safe from snowdrifts and passing herds. In spring, getting the pasture ready for cattle was as simple as lifting the wires up and clipping them back to the posts.

Once, I set out early to work my way around a let-down fence that started above the barn and headed west until it met a big ridge. Turning south from there, the fence climbed for miles toward the ridgeline. The whole pasture was tilted, and the top rose high enough to be visible from almost anywhere in the valley.

I can't remember why I started at the bottom of the hill. Maybe I thought I could use the exercise. More likely it was too early in the morning to do any thinking at all. Either way I left the four-wheeler at the gate, grabbed my fencing pliers, buckled on a tool belt full of extra insulators and staples, and headed for the first post.

The routine was simple: walk to the post, reach out with the pliers, yank the pin from one of the insulators, stoop, lift the wire, slip it into the insulator, and slam the pin home. I repeated the process for each wire, and then moved on to the next post in the line. I got good at this, and quick enough so that from a distance it must have looked like I was paying my respects to a receiving line of posts—bowing three times and then moving on.

Fixing fence would be a lot easier if it didn't involve bending over all the time. Because I'm relatively tall, my back always wears out first. I tried to extend its useful life with little tricks like dropping onto one knee while I clipped the bottom wire or developing shortcuts that let me straighten up a fraction sooner on each post. Perfecting these strategies usually distracted me from the pain and repetition.

Sometimes the pins were missing, so I replaced them with crimped, two-inch fencing staples. Every so often an insulator was torn away or chewed to a nub. I pulled a new one from a pocket on my tool belt and stapled it up, wondering what creature ate insulators and why.

Slowly, over the course of a few hours, I climbed halfway up the hill. It was one of those clear, early season days that starts out cold enough to sting your lungs and then blossoms into something like summer. The sun had come up in a clear blue sky and the new, raw light of spring scorched the pasture. It flashed off the wires, making me squint and stumble. Conspiring with the pasture's slope, the sun warmed me until I itched beneath my jacket and my face beaded with sweat.

I would have taken off my coat and left it hanging on the fence, but the shape of the pasture and my plans for the day were such that I would pass each spot only once. Returning for the jacket would have meant walking far out of my way, so I kept it on and labored up the line, stewing.

But as I sweated my way uphill, everything began to go haywire: a pin wouldn't pop free of the insulator, and then it wouldn't slide back in; a staple twisted as I pounded it with the fencing pliers, splitting the post; I picked up the middle wire when I wanted the top one and strung a dozen posts before I noticed the mistake; the wires twisted together so I had to walk up and down the hill to unwind them, yanking in different directions and pinching my fingers.

At the midway point I was thoroughly browbeaten. I no longer looked uphill to see what was ahead of me, or down to check how far I had come. My attention shifted from the ground to the post and back again, that was all. It was a shame: less than a month on the ranch and already the work was breaking me.

It took me a while to realize that I had reached the top. I might have crossed the crest without looking up, except I came to a braced corner, glanced past it, and found myself staring out across what seemed an endless void.

I stood on the ridge's end. Beyond me the ground dropped precipitously away toward where the Madison River ran north for miles in its willow cradle. The winding course of it was framed on either side by mountains and was darker blue than the sky. For a moment, in spite of the sweat in my eyes or because of it, I saw the land more clearly than I ever had, and it was beautiful.

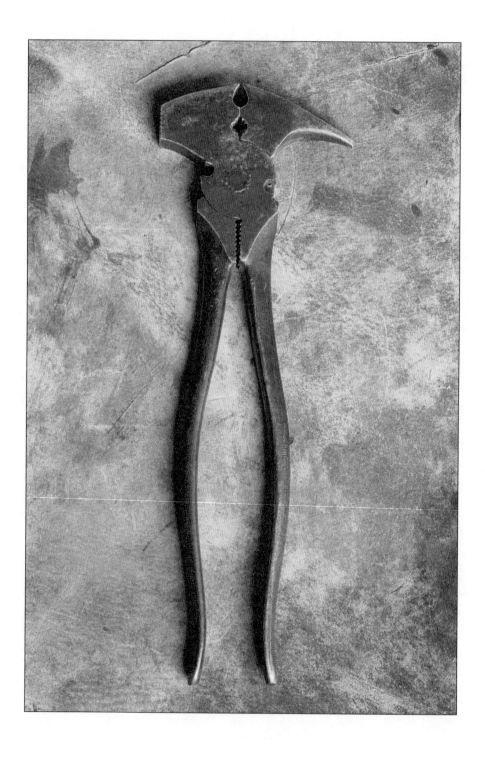

– II –

THE WORK

Bad Luck

*T*he stockman Orville Skogen arrived at the head of a convoy of cattle trucks, leaped down to the ground, and started barking greetings and orders in quick succession. He stuck out a stubby, powerful hand for Jeremy to shake and yelled at one of his drivers to back up to a portable loading chute. James and I were horseback, watching from a distance in the pasture as the first load of cattle poured off the truck. Steers banged down the metal ramp, took a flying leap onto the grass, and then trotted toward us. There seemed to be an impossible number of them in the trailer. Once a couple dozen got into the pasture, they began to mill and bunch against the fences. James and I rode back and forth to keep them together and calm. Orville and Jeremy stood on either side of the chute, counting animals with little flicking motions of their hands. Every so often Orville would shake his head at a thin steer or nod approvingly at a fat one. Both motions set his jowls trembling, like a bulldog worrying a bone.

Orville's cattle were a motley bunch. Some ranchers take pride in the genetics of their herd and breed carefully through the years toward a particular conformation or an ideal amount of marbling in the meat. The family line is an inheritance, passed through generations of cows and cowboys. If it earns a reputation, the calves will fetch a higher price.

With the cattle he brought to the Sun, Orville preferred to make his money by the pound. He cruised stock sales every fall, buying calves by the lot. After a winter's worth of growth, the calves matured into yearlings. Orville made sure all his steers were properly castrated, and he spayed most of his heifers, too, since sterile animals spend less time screwing and more time eating. In late spring, he brought his vast herds out to places like the Sun Ranch for the grazing season. When fall rolled around, he hauled them to feedlots in the Midwest or sold them for slaughter.

On the ranch we charged fifty cents per head per day for all the grass a yearling could eat. In the right conditions, grass became flesh at a rate of two or three pounds per day. Since cattle sold at around a dollar per pound and there were more than one hundred days in the grazing season, Orville's operation made a lot of economic sense.

The trucks took turns at the loading chute, each disgorging all manner of steers: Charolais, Red and Black Angus, Simmental, Hereford, and every crossbreed in between. When the last steer stepped off the ramp, we let the herd spill past us. They trotted uphill and we followed, driving them toward tall grass, salt tubs, and water. The steers didn't move easily. Nervous and squirrely from their long interstate haul, they shoved each other and looked for routes of escape. Conscious of the fact that Jeremy and Orville were standing by the trailer watching, James and I rode angles back and forth behind the stragglers, zigzagging our way up-country. When an animal broke off the left side of the herd, I chased it down, turned it, and hustled it back in the right direction. On his side, James did the same. One of James's younger stock dogs trotted gamely along with us, nipping occasionally at the heels of lagging cattle.

When we got back to the trucks and the ramp, Orville stopped complaining about beef prices, his bottom line, and the goddamn wolves long enough to shake my hand.

—————•—•—•—————

After the cows arrived, our days started at 6:30, or earlier if we had to move a herd. I rolled from bed, fumbled through a shower, and ate whatever was close to hand in the kitchen. At the window I looked out to read the thermometer. Most early-June mornings the temperature hovered between twenty and thirty degrees Fahrenheit.

We spread the cattle across the ranch according to our grazing plan. There were two large herds: one of 680 steers and the other of 790 heifers. Both belonged to Orville Skogen. In addition to the yearlings, we pastured 200 cow-calf pairs from a family ranch down by Ennis.

Once, I talked with the matriarch of that family—a silver-haired, no-bullshit woman—when she came to drop off her cattle. She was on horseback and I was afoot, and somehow we got started on the subject of wolves. She had heard rumblings about the new incarnation of the Taylor Peak Pack, now called the Wedge Pack, which sounded like trouble.

"How do you figure," she asked, "to keep them out of my cattle?"

I told her, as Jeremy had so often told me, that we were going to do everything in our power to keep the worst from happening. We would patrol the herd diligently, I said, and track the collared wolves in the pack with a telemetry system on loan from the University of Montana. When the two groups of animals got too close together, we would haze the wolves back into the wilderness and sleep out beside the cattle.

I went on, warming to my task: We had nonlethal shotgun loads—cracker shells and rubber bullets. We had an experimental contraption called fladry, a one-string fence of twine and plastic flagging that was thought to frighten wolves. When her cows and calves moved into the riskiest places, we would ring their pasture with fladry and monitor the results. The hope, I told her, was to keep the cattle safe and learn something new about coexisting with predators.

She took this in, listening with her mouth set in a grim line. When I finished talking, she let the silence hang long between us. Finally, she spoke:

"You're going to put a string of flags around the cows?"

That was the plan, I said.

"How does that keep the wolves out?"

I confessed that I didn't exactly know, but we had reports of it working well to protect sheep herds in Europe.

She let more silence pass, and then asked me if I owned a gun.

I mentioned my newly acquired pump shotgun and reminded her about the cracker shells and rubber slugs.

"No," she said. "A real gun, a rifle. With bullets."

When I told her I didn't own a rifle, she stared at me as though I had revealed a deep-seated, appalling vice. Looking down from the saddle, she fixed me with a hard, appraising glare. It got to me. For a moment I was ashamed to be a man of twenty-three, presenting myself as a ranch hand, with just a shotgun to my name.

As she watched me think this through, her face softened just a fraction.

"Tell you what," she said. "If you need a gun, you call me."

"Thank you," I replied. "I'll keep it in mind."

"Do that," she said. "We'll get you what you need for the wolves."

She spun her horse and rode away, leaving me among her family's cattle.

———•◦•———

With our summer herds settled and grazing on the ranch, my own life fell into a reassuring, exhausting rhythm. Each morning, unless we were scheduled to move a herd from one pasture to another, I filled a couple of gas cans, strapped them to a four-wheeler, and buzzed uphill along the paired wheel ruts that followed Moose Creek toward the mountains. On the way up, I drove past each stock tank, checking to make sure the floats worked and the water was high. Mobs of steers scattered before me, and I scanned the herd for signs of lameness or trouble. When I saw a suspicious limp or swelling, I recorded it in a little red stock book that

Jeremy had given me. The books came free from a company that sold feed supplements. Mine was small enough to fit in a breast pocket and said "Vigortone" on the cover. It was wonderfully organized, with dated, boxed-out spaces for describing ailments, animals, and treatments. Jeremy probably filled them in correctly, but I just picked a random page, scrawled something like "Black Baldy with foot rot on left hind," and finished with a barely legible notation of the tag number.

I puttered uphill, roughly following our water line until I reached the top of the pasture and a massive, circular cistern. Although it had been painted brown to match the grass, the tank looked rude and industrial against the foothills. Not far from its base, a generator and a wellhead sat inside a small fenced enclosure. I boosted one of the cans across the fence, leaped over, and began to tinker with the generator.

We had two of these setups, one on either side of Moose Creek. The wells were capable of bringing up nine or ten gallons per minute, the tanks held fifty-seven hundred gallons each, and pipes led downhill to more than a dozen stock tanks.

The average cow on good pasture drinks ten to twelve gallons each day, which meant our steers sucked around 8,160 gallons from the ground seven days a week. The heifer herd required even more, totaling approximately 9,480 daily gallons. Keeping pace with these demands meant running the generators for up to fourteen hours a day during the grazing season.

It would have been simpler to water our herds from the creek. We could have fenced our pastures so the creek ran right through the middle of them, dumped in a load of cattle, and called it good. That's the easy way, and the old way. The stock gets its own water, and nobody has to set tanks or run pipe or bounce across a washboard road to stoke a generator. But cattle are hell on creeks and the ground around them. They loiter by the banks and foul the water. If left to their own devices and not rotated through pastures quickly enough, they chew the riparian grass to nothing. Naked banks slump into the water, and soon the creek is destroyed, gone, replaced by a barren, deeply incised gully. We fought against this process all over the ranch, adding off-stream water sources to the most heavily used fields. In other, more remote pastures, we used a combination of temporary electric fence and vigorous herding to keep the cattle on the move and away from the most fragile areas.

Our system of tanks, pipe, and pumps was built to take the pressure off natural water sources and it worked pretty well. The only real problem was the amount of gasoline and maintenance required to keep it going. Fourteen hours a day is a lot to ask of an old motor, especially when it's kept outside and chilled below freezing every night.

I fussed with the generator, adding oil and picking grass seeds from the air filter. After filling the empty gas tank to the brim and adjusting the choke to its sweet spot, I reached down and pulled on the starter cord for all I was worth. The generator rattled, coughed, and died. I yanked the cord frantically, until the skin of my palm started to burn. When the generator kicked over, I stood beside it panting. I ran a hand across my forehead to clear off the day's first sweat.

I almost always started mornings like that: up along the cold, roiling creek, then north across a bumpy stretch of sagebrush to the mouth of Bad Luck Canyon. We had a spring box there, built to siphon water out of Bad Luck Creek and send it downhill to a line of tanks that dotted an otherwise dry section of the ranch. Although it was sunk in one of the stream's slower, deeper holes and ringed around with a couple different sizes of wire mesh, the box trapped silt, old leaves, and debris. I shoveled it out almost every day, and then reamed the box's intake holes with a stick. By the time I had the water running strong, my hands would be frozen stiff. I'd lean against the four-wheeler and try to slap some life back into them.

The spring box sat high on the ranch, near the foot of the Madisons, so that gravity could do the work of moving water. Building it there was a utilitarian decision; the spot's sweeping view was incidental. Still, it stopped me in my tracks every day. Downhill, toward the west and the river, the valley spread out for miles. In the foreground, the new green grass looked soft as a carpet. It shimmered with each gust of wind. The two movie-set cabins punctuated the middle distance, lonely, gray, and weathered. Anyone who didn't know the story behind them would have thought they had stood there for a century or more.

I usually began to take in the landscape by looking west, the friendlier panorama, across the valley toward the faraway Gravelly Range, letting the rising sun warm my back. But I always turned east and stared up the course of the creek to where it spilled out of the mountains at Bad Luck Canyon. Jeremy said the canyon belonged to the wolves. It was narrow and full of bones, the sides so steep a man couldn't climb them without using his hands.

"Predator alley," he said. "It'll make your hair stand on end."

The mouth of the canyon was thick with trees on its south slope and framed by two sharply angled hillsides, like a Newhouse trap with its jaws splayed out, waiting for a footfall on the pan. Although the hills didn't look very steep from the spring box, they still had a menacing aspect. I strained my eyes to see past the spot where the walls came together in a massive V, but couldn't penetrate the foliage and shadow.

Such dark places were magnetic. I felt the same pull at the mouth of a cave, a mine shaft, a bog, or any obscure place that I had been warned about explicitly. On wild, moonless nights, the darkness called me away from the safe circle of firelight, challenging me to transgress, to step beyond my world into an ancient, unforgiving one.

My curiosity about Bad Luck Canyon got the best of me one Saturday, when my only job that day was to make rounds of the generators and clean out the spring box. When finished, I left the four-wheeler and walked uphill along the creek. I didn't own a pistol then, and hadn't thought to bring a can of bear spray, so I went up Bad Luck Creek armed with a pair of fencing pliers. I held them with the staple hook pointing forward, an agricultural war club.

The wind stopped when I passed into the mountains. It got dark, too, since the Madisons now blocked the sun. I stopped beneath a good-sized pine to catch my breath and let my eyes adjust. When they did, I looked down to find the first skeleton.

The elk calf lay on the uphill side of the tree with its spine bent backward to match the curve of the trunk. Its ribs were gone, snapped off clean as wishbones. The long bones of the leg were cracked in half and the skull was missing. Rough incisions marred the unbroken bones. Not a shred of skin remained, but the ground was scattered with a halo of fur that I recognized as the wolf's particular calling card.

The creek was small, no wider than a long stride. Following it uphill, I stepped over a shocking multitude of bones. Spines lay like snakes in the grass, and disarticulated vertebrae dotted the ground like strange, low weeds. I stopped to study the fresher kills, the ones still held together by bits of dried black sinew, and found the brutal strength of wolves recorded in bone shear.

A quarter mile back was a little shack as thoroughly disassembled as the skeletons. I tripped over a griddle and found a stovepipe, a wringer, and bedsprings scattered near the open door. Inside, a caved-in roof divided the cabin in half. One side was littered with gnawed bones.

As I climbed, my worries multiplied. Game trails snaked along the bottom of the canyon. Spurs departed at intervals to climb awhile and peter out in scree. Looking back downhill, I found that I could no longer see the sunlit floor of the valley, or even the faraway green hump of the Gravelly Range. My world was ringed with dark, impenetrable timber, punctuated by the dull white of weathering bone, and bounded on two sides by slopes that had grown steeper until they looked impossible to ascend.

I turned a corner and hopped once more across the canyon's little cataract. As I landed on the other side, a tremendous racket issued from one of the nearer trees. It happened fast—a series of quick, dull explosions, like a string of fireworks held underwater. The noise was loud, close, and terrifying. I froze in my tracks, with my heart beating hard enough to hear. Even when a blue grouse emerged from the branches and coasted away down the canyon with its wings still making a bizarre flooded-engine sound, I couldn't relax.

Bad Luck had that effect on people—and livestock, too. In an old, unpublished history of the Madison Valley, I had read about the etymology of all the creeks around here. For most streams the naming process was mundane. Moose and Wolf Creeks were named for animals seen on their banks, apparently by men without a surfeit of creativity. Down the valley, Meadow Creek took its name from the wide expanse of grass through which it meandered. Of Squaw Creek, the author wrote only that the drainage contained the graves of horse thieves, killed by a posse of deputies from Gallatin City.

But Bad Luck Creek was different. Bad Luck had a story. In the very early days, when homesteads were being proved up around Ennis and the first big ranches had yet to be pieced together in the upper valley, a man rode his horse up into the bowels of a little drainage near Moose Creek. Like me, the man crossed and recrossed the little brook in the center of the canyon, stepping over enough bone piles to put his mount on edge.

High in the canyon, the man caught sight of a grouse sitting nearby in a tree. Grouse have two major challenges when it comes to their survival: First, they're delicious, easily cooked on an open fire, and about the right size to make a hearty lunch. Second, they tend to overestimate their ability to blend in to their surroundings and will sit motionless on a tree branch until a person is nearly within arm's reach.

Seeing the grouse, the man dismounted. He picked up one of the blocky stones that litter the canyon floor and led his horse toward the bird. When he judged himself close enough, he chucked the stone with all his strength. It missed, but not by much, and the grouse leaped from the tree in a riot of motion and sound, flapping between man and animal, nearly brushing them with its wings.

The noise, the bird, the smells of decay, and the carcass piles did not sit well with the horse, which reared back, broke free of the man, and ran downhill as fast as it could go. It did not stop to graze or drink, but kept going, out of the canyon, across Stock Creek and the vastness of the North End, and on down the valley to Ennis.

The man, for his part, walked out. He wanted to call the drainage Grouse Creek, but his friends overruled him, calling it Bad Luck. Because of all the bones and how the place gets under a person's skin, the name stuck.

It isn't wise to ruminate for too long in a place like that, but it's tempting. I was totally and utterly alone. Standing in the high green grass along the creek and thinking about the man who named creek and canyon, I got lost in the strangeness of Bad Luck and its weird, dangerous vibe. After a few minutes, a little stone broke loose from some unseen talus patch, clattered down the hill, and splashed into the creek behind me. The noise startled me, but still I headed higher.

After a mile, the stream forked. Neither tributary was much more than a trickle, and both spilled from steep, uphill gashes in the canyon walls. Although it was nearly noon, the canyon's floor remained in shadow. It felt like a dead end—a place built perfectly for ambush—and reminded me of a painting that hung in Roger's house. On the canvas a massive, exhausted bull elk struggles to keep three snarling wolves at bay. The bull stands in a dark little clearing with his back to a thick stand of timber, looking ready to collapse beneath the weight of his antlers. The wolves watch him intently, waiting for their cue to begin the final act.

I listened to the faint tune of Bad Luck Creek and nudged at a heap of old rib bones with the toe of my boot. A breeze came out from the high country, cold enough to make me shiver, and I followed it downhill toward the light and safety of the valley floor.

———•◦•———

There was a place near the river and the highway, at the foot of a steep, barren hill, where elk always seemed to get into trouble. On an otherwise unremarkable little mound, the remnants of an old, salty spring rose to the surface. Nothing much grew where the little vein of minerals popped out into daylight, but it drew the elk and deer in all seasons, especially in the dead of winter, when exposure and the passage of time had leached most of the nutrition out of the bunchgrasses. During the months of January, February, and March the salt lick invariably held a crowd of deer and elk with their noses pressed against the chalky, pulverized dirt, ingesting the salt, potassium, magnesium, sulfur, and iron they needed to carry on.

In ungulates, as in other mammals, salt engenders a powerful thirst. After grubbing their fill at the lick, elk and deer would lift their heads and hear the soft gurgle of water moving down the Madison River. Wide and relatively slow there, the river was irresistible. But even though the Madison was no more than two hundred yards from the lick, crossing the distance between the two was treacherous, and our boundary fence was a significant obstacle. Near the salt lick, that fence was a stout affair: four tight strands of smooth, high-tensile wire mounted on closely spaced wooden posts. The fence's bottom wire was about a foot off the ground, and its top one pushed fifty inches. For elk, crossing it meant a high-stakes leap. Over the course of my time on the Sun, I would find several for whom it had ended badly.

———

A small, calm bunch of elk generally had little trouble crossing fences. They took their time, scoped out the line, picked a good spot, and leaped cleanly over with a grace surprising for their size. Trouble cropped up when the herds were larger or began to hurry. In big bunches the elk jostled together, roughly pushing each other forward. As animals at the back of the herd pressed ahead, the ones up front had to leap the fence or be shoved through it.

When the herd got spooked, the danger was compounded. With a wolf or a hunter behind them, the elk ran pell-mell through anything in their path. In such moments of panic, the herd tried to steamroller over the boundary fence with disastrous results. Most of the animals made the leap cleanly or flicked their hooves across the top wire. Others fell short, bouncing off the fence or wedging themselves through the spaces in between strands. These were the fortunate ones. A luckless few jumped, ended up with a leg or two stuck between the wires, and, carried ahead by their own momentum, pitched over the top of the fence. As an elk twisted the fence out of shape, the wires bound against each other and tightened like a vise.

From there on out, it got ugly. The elk struggled violently to get loose, and sometimes made a frenzied, bloody escape. But when the wires were twisted, steel tightened above their hooves as surely as a leghold trap. As they kicked, it sliced through hide, muscle, and ligament, right down to the bone.

Once, while out working, I spooked a little bunch of elk and watched all but one of them make it across a pasture fence. The last cow got a hind leg tangled badly and began to fight against the wire. I ran to the fence, got as close as I dared, and cut her free. She limped away, bleeding just a little.

Such happy endings weren't normal. Mostly, the carnage went on without a witness. Once caught and irreparably damaged by fighting against tempered metal, the elk waited awkwardly to die. Some bled out; others were claimed by exposure. Wolves and bears found a few and tore them limb from ruined limb. More than once, while repairing remote barbwire fences in the spring-time, I found the hooves and shanks of ungulates still twisted in the wires.

We worked hard to keep the animals from such grisly ends. Before I arrived, the ranch had already replaced miles of high, hazardous barbwire fence with more wildlife-friendly designs. When we built new fences, they were generally low and electri-fied, standing no more than forty inches off the ground. Since they carried current enough to keep our stock in check, the new fences could be strung relatively loosely, on flexible fiberglass posts. Deer and elk could cross them easily, fluidly—almost without breaking stride.

The boundary fence by the lick was a necessary exception. Highway 287 dropped off a steep grade there, and then swung through a blind corner. When the temperature dropped below freezing, steam rose off the river and glazed the road with a slick of ice. We lived in fear of livestock getting loose, ending up on the highway, and causing a massive wreck, so we kept the boundary fence high, tight, and impeccably maintained.

One day, while checking that fence where it cut through a little grove of willows, I found a casualty in the wires. In spite of time, rot, and partial disarticulation, the elk's body had remained tan-gled. Most of her flesh was gone, torn away by scavengers, leaving the ribs out and gray as old snowdrifts. The remaining skin and hair were falling away in loose, disintegrating sheets. Her body sagged down from the fence at a gut-wrenching angle, with its skull cocked grotesquely to the side.

The elk had been badly, hopelessly stuck, with her hind legs pinched between the second and third wires. To complicate matters, she had somehow managed to flip several times over the fence, snugging the wires down farther with every rotation. The result was a disconcertingly neat, perfectly symmetrical bow-tie shape with two elk legs at dead center.

I pulled a bow saw from the fencing bucket I carried and began to work. The cutting went quicker than I thought it would—three hacks across a joint split the first leg. The other yielded similarly, and the wires twanged back into position, spinning the two grisly shanks high into the air. I stepped back, breathing through my mouth to avoid the smell of death. The wires of the fence were perfectly straight and totally unmarred. When I returned later in the season on another errand, the elk's remains were gone and no sign of the violence remained.

Calluses

*A*fter a hurried lunch, I had loaded all sorts of fencing tools into my work truck and headed out to fix a handful of broken H-braces on a fence at the ranch's South End. An H-brace, as the name suggests, consists of two upright posts, usually eight feet apart, with a stout rail spanning the distance between them. Such braces are the capstone of every good barbwire fence. They stand at corners, on hilltops, and in swales, holding fast against the tension of the wires. An H-brace is pinned together by a pair of heavy spikes, which are driven through the posts and into each end of the rail. This, however, is not what gives the contraption its strength.

An H-brace is a masterpiece of applied physics. Properly built, it stands as strong as rock and stays that way for decades. The secret is in the wire: Picture the low H of the brace's wooden frame. Upon it, superimpose an equally wide X formed of two loops of wire. One loop connects the lower left and upper right corners of the brace. The other angles from lower right to upper left. At either end, the loops are secured to the posts with fencing staples.

To get to the broken braces, I had to cover just over three miles as the crow flies. In the truck, however, the trip was circuitous and excruciatingly slow. I bounced over glacial boulders that studded all the ranch's high pastures and sloshed through little springs that turned the dirt into a soupy mess. With the truck groaning in four-wheel drive, I skidded uphill to a windswept ridge with a sweeping vista of Squaw Creek's timbered crenulations.

The braces were in a particularly inconvenient spot, where the land dropped off steeply and the fence turned often to stay on level ground. By the time I pulled up at the first one and looked at the dashboard clock, the trip had taken nearly an hour.

For the most part, I could tell very quickly how long digging postholes would take and how difficult it would be. If the shovel, when stabbed down, slid into the ground a few inches with a satisfying crunch, the dirt was cooperative. If, on the other hand, it clanged like an off-pitch bell and bounced back through my hands, hard hours were in the offing.

At the first brace, I stomped on the shovel, giving it all I had to little avail. A spasm of all-out work yielded just a six-inch crater around the old post. I looked down the line at the rotten, shattered braces that needed to be dismantled, dug out, and replaced. I was in for a long afternoon.

Setting aside my shovel, I pulled a rock bar from the back of the truck. A simple, brutish tool made for unforgiving soil, the bar we had on the Sun Ranch was a heavy steel rod, six feet long and tipped at one end with a flat, tempered blade that looked like an oversized flathead screwdriver. The blade was used for shattering rock and dry, compacted earth into pieces that could be shoveled out. The bar's other end terminated in a thick, three-inch disk of steel for tamping earth back in around a newly set post.

The rock bar was never fun to use. It weighed twenty pounds and tended to peel the skin from my palms with shocking efficiency. But the bar was often the only way to get the job done.

I beat steel against embedded stones until they broke or loosened, mining downward. Every few minutes, I scooped out loose material with the shovel and piled it at the edge of my excavation.

The first hole took half an hour. When the old post finally broke loose, I tossed it away and sat panting like an overheated dog. Sweat rolled down my face, cutting lines through the accumulated dust and dirt. I set a new post, checked its position with a level, and tamped the dirt back in around it.

I repeated that process on the brace's other end—toiled down, set the post, filled the hole—and then bent myself to the work of rebuilding the brace. After nailing up a rail between the posts, I strung loops of wire and then tightened them by sticking a short piece of wood, perhaps two feet long, through the center of the X they made. As I twisted the wood in circles, the wires began to wrap around each other. They grew taut as guitar strings and the wood groaned under the strain.

That's where I stopped. Pushed too far, this massive tension will snap wire, break rails, and unseat the bases of the posts from the ground. I set the twister against the rail and pinned it there with a framing nail. I kicked the brace as hard as I could, and it didn't budge. Satisfied, I spliced the barbwire of the fence together and stapled it to each new post.

I looked down the line at the work yet to be done. The sun was falling toward the western edge of the sky, the afternoon passing quickly. I gathered my tools and went back to the truck, shook off my work gloves, and reached into the cab for my water bottle. After drinking deeply from it, I noticed my hands were stained an unnatural yellow. Sweat had mobilized whatever noxious chemical was used to tan my gloves and it had stained my skin a dead, unsettling hue. It worried me, so I flipped my hands over to have a look at the palms. They looked even worse. In addition to being yellow, my palms were torn to pieces. A number of calluses, softened by sweat or the tanning agent, had torn loose. The raw, new skin beneath them oozed clear liquid with a slight red tint. I peeled off the biggest sloughed pieces and threw them in the grass at my feet.

As I looked down at the jaundiced wreckage of my palms, I felt a strange surge of pride. These weren't city boy hands. They weren't delicate by a long shot. From the elbows down, the skin of my arms was covered with a chiaroscuro of barbwire scratches. The older ones had healed, peeled, and turned a dark, bluish color from the sun. More recent marks were zippered shut with lines of cracking scab. A few spots, either sliced today or bumped hard enough to reopen, were smeared with small patches of freshly dried blood.

In Thailand young men who train to be kickboxers beat their legs against trees for hours on end. Their shins fill up with ugly welts, and bones break if they push too far beyond the limits of physiology. After a while, they can hardly feel the impact. They fight serenely on, comfortable in the knowledge that most of their relevant nerves have already been beaten to death, and the ones left over are too worn-out to protest much. Their notion of pain, once sharp as a blade, has been worn down by long effort, until it is as smooth as a river stone. Ranching is similar.

The real work of ranching isn't riding horses, moving cattle, shoveling shit, fixing fence, digging holes, or any other specific task. It is instead the process of toughening the body into something worn, weathered, scarred, and strong enough to do everything asked of it, and honing the mind until it knows precisely what it can and should ask of the body.

I got in the truck, drove down the line, and built another brace while all the shadows lengthened. I built a third in the failing glow of dusk. Not far from the last brace, I found a dried-out pile of wolf shit in the sage. I chopped it apart with the rock bar, and a little cloud of undigested elk hair rose into the evening breeze.

I turned the truck for home, picking my way along the rough track, paying close attention to the shapes that passed through the edges of the headlights. I hoped for elk, deer, or a fleeting glimpse of some loping predator, but nothing appeared except scrub brush and the rolling land. Looking closely at an old, sagging fence that crossed the road, I could not help thinking that the forces of time and weather were already at work on the braces I had built.

Though the posts were set well and the wires tightly strained, the long process of their decay had begun. A decade would find them gray and rusting. In a century they would be all but gone—toppled in the grass and picked apart by endless freeze and thaw. Elk would step carefully across the ruins of my best efforts. Sagebrush would rise to hide the braces, as they did the myriad piles of old bones that dotted the ranch's pastures. In time, the last traces of my labor would dissolve into the dirt, leaving only wild animals, hardy plants, and the wide blue sky.

———•◦•———

The following Sunday morning, just a few days after I finished shredding my palms in the course of building fence braces, I checked the stock tanks and the salt tubs, and then went walking. I parked the four-wheeler at the upper fence of one of the ranch's highest pastures and hiked up the road that curled like a cow's tongue around the low end of the Squaw Creek hogback. June was in its final days, and in places the grass had grown tall enough to brush against my outstretched, swinging fingertips.

Earlier in the week James, Jeremy, and I had piled into the truck cab together and driven up Badluck Way. Distracted, I'd stared into the rearview mirror and watched Jeremy's dogs run back and forth on the flatbed. Just after we emerged from the Moose Creek canyon, Jeremy pointed out toward an ocean of grass and sage and said: "Wolf!"

A moment later James saw it, too. I stared for all I was worth, but I couldn't see anything but grass and brush. They pointed it out and gave me landmarks, but still I peered intently and saw—nothing. Soon they let me know it had dropped from sight. It would be just my luck, I thought, to work a summer here and never see a wolf.

But sign was everywhere. I couldn't walk through an open gate or turn the corner of a fence line without running into evidence of wolves. Paw prints snaked across muddy spots in the road, each one the size of a man's fist. Most of the gateposts were spattered with piss. Black, hair-rich piles of scat dotted all the well-worn trails.

Talk of wolves abounded, too. Neighboring ranchers, hunting guides, and people from town reminded me often of the grisly possibilities that waited in the months ahead. I heard about calves gone missing, horses that came home wild-eyed and bloody, and all those goats a few years ago, turned out to graze noxious weeds in the foothills and never seen again.

Once, on a four-wheeler, I nearly ran over the carcass of an elk calf. Its chest and stomach were torn wide open, the ribs inside broken off cleanly. Blood was everywhere, matting the grass and coagulated in dark, gelatinous pools. The rumen and intestines lay nearby in the sage. Organs were missing. I toed the body and found that it was not yet stiff. I put my hand against the neck and it was warm.

I didn't see the wolves, but they must have been watching. When I came back in the evening, nothing remained of the calf except the usual scattered hair and bones.

As I climbed up the Squaw Creek hogback, I briefly pictured the calf's gaping abdomen. Then I put it from my mind because the weather was so good, and I was determined to enjoy a rare moment of recreation.

———

What we called a hogback was really the last ridge of the mountains—a moraine left over from glacial times. It sprawled out from the base of the Madisons and struck south for about half a mile. Its west side, which faced the lower pastures of the ranch, was steep and rocky. I expected the east side to look similar.

It didn't. Hidden behind the hogback was a vast, gently sloping bowl of grass. It was dotted with small, regularly shaped swellings in the ground, scaled like the ones on golf courses. On its far side, the bowl ended at a wall of close-set trees that marked the beginning of the Lee Metcalf Wilderness's 250,000 acres of stone peaks, alpine lakes, and seldom-traveled trails.

I hiked uphill toward the gorgeous, rock-sided slit in the mountains that gave birth to Squaw Creek. Low clouds blew in from the southwest, and the canyon gobbled them up.

I am tempted to say that the wolf caught the corner of my eye. It would be simplest if I had noticed something, and then turned my head to see. That makes sense, but it isn't the truth. Telling it that way gets the order wrong. What really happened was this: I felt movement. Something rose up from the back of my skull, climbed my brainstem quick as lightning, and spun my head around.

Wolf. I knew before my eyes found it near the tree line. It was tall, slim-legged, and gray, with a tail like a sickle. I did not think, Coyote, for a second. It wasn't maybe. There was no shred of doubt.

I knew my job. Not long ago I'd stood with James and Jeremy and listened to a couple of Fish, Wildlife & Parks employees hash out the basics of wolf deterrence. Mike, the valley's wolf biologist, explained the finer points of the law: since the wolves had been intentionally reintroduced to the Yellowstone by the United States

Fish and Wildlife Service, they were treated slightly differently than most animals protected by the Endangered Species Act. The main rule, known as 10(j) in legal documents, allowed us to non-lethally harass the wolves whenever they came near our livestock. Once they started to chase cattle, sheep, horses, or any other domesticated species, we could shoot for real.

Mike brought out a shotgun with the butt wrapped in red tape and showed us how to fire noisemaker shells. After loading the gun with rubber slugs, he let us take shots at a wolf-sized piece of half-inch plywood. James went first and missed. My slug knocked a quarter-sized hole in the wood.

"The box says 'less than lethal' instead of 'nonlethal' for a reason," Mike said. "These aren't for shooting each other in the ass with."

He talked about our resident wolves, the Wedge Pack. They numbered nine this year, not including the pups born early in spring. Mike had two radios in the pack, but hoped to trap and collar more animals during the summer. Once the wolves had gotten established, the current incarnation of the Wedge Pack had grown quickly. In addition to raising at least two healthy litters of pups, Mike suspected that it had absorbed a few "dispersers," wolves that had wandered in solo, found a place within the pack, and decided to stay. That was the great and damning thing about wolf biology—given an ample prey base and enough room to roam, they spread easily across the landscape. With an average litter size between four and seven pups, two wolves became a dozen in very short order. This didn't bode well in a valley like the Madison, with thousands of cattle wandering the foothills.

To stay alive and fit, a good-sized wolf pack needs to kill an elk or something like it every few days. The birth of each new, hungry pup increases the pressure to kill large animals, a task that grows harder as the snowpack melts and elk move into the highest reaches of the mountains. By early summer, the south end of the Madison was already buzzing with rumors of depredation. In the mountains above Sun West, cowboys had found a Black Angus calf dead in a ring of blood and scattered hair, its bones cracked for marrow and scattered. Wolves had been seen chasing livestock on another neighboring ranch, so they were the prime suspects. Mike ran some numbers in his head and he didn't like the results.

"With that many wolves on the ranch," he said, "you're probably going to have a problem."

At the end Mike paused for questions.

"What if I see a wolf and don't have a gun?" I asked him.

"Yell and chase it as far as you can."

I stood on the hogback, remembering his advice. Cattle were already grazing on the lower pastures of the ranch, and the Wedge Pack had a rap sheet of suspected depredations. Making them fear the sound, sight, and smell of man was our best hope for a peaceful summer.

In spite of all that, I did nothing. I stood frozen until the wolf moved. It stepped forward, broke into a loose-limbed trot, and followed the edge of the forest. The world was quiet. The weather was calm. The wolf traveled smooth as a ghost for a few seconds, then turned left and disappeared in the trees.

My hands shook a little. The air seemed colder. I suspected that there might be consequences.

One night in midwinter, a waxing moon shone across the North End, glowing bone white on the grass and throwing long shadows behind the ruins of old homestead buildings. The air was clear, with a crystalline, breathless quality that comes only when the temperature falls well below zero. A southeast wind had been at work, shoveling snow across the Flats and stashing it in the lee of anything that stood off the ground.

The elk were restless and swirled like a shoal of fish. Wheeling into the wind, they headed for shelter in the aspen groves near Wolf Creek. Earlier in the night, just after twilight gave out and the moon reared up in the east, they heard the wolves howling back in the Madisons. Later, over the hissing snow and grass, they heard them again from somewhere closer. Moving across the plain, the elk stretched out into a ragged column. A handful of the older cows went first, picking their way through the scattered glacial cobble. Then came the hoi polloi, the vast, dark majority of the herd. Innumerable cows, calves, and young spike bulls bunched together against the cold and the night. The big bulls stayed mostly toward the rear, following the herd and nodding their weighty racks at the stars.

The elk were still on the move when the wolves came loping out of the Mounds. Since its origins in the union of a single breeding pair, the Wedge Pack had come into its prime: a half dozen mature wolves raced down from the hills, trailed at a little distance by a handful of yearling pups. They pressed forward, scattering elk like leaves before a hard wind.

Most of the herd turned back the way they had come. They balled up in a huge, tight scrum and beat a path back to the safety of the open, windswept North End. The wolves let them go.

A smaller bunch ran south. They raced down through the creek, breaking ice, stumbling across slick, round stones, and fighting through close-grown stands of willow. The wolves were on their heels as they pounded up a little hill and across the plain. There, on flat and frozen ground, the wolves struggled to keep from falling behind. The elk stretched out and ran for all they were worth, leaping sage and blowing through the little piles of snow that form behind each tuft of bunchgrass. They found a frantic rhythm in their flight, and it carried them forward. The lead cows knew the country well. They stared ahead at the long, steep slope of the Stock Creek bench, knowing that if they made the top, the wolves could not keep pace with them forever.

In a burst of strength, the elk began to climb. They labored up through snow that deepened until it overtopped the grass and sage. They blew clouds of steam in the moonlight. The wolves followed in their tracks.

The Stock Creek bench is a hard climb in any season—it is steep, scattered with loose rocks, and long enough to make you wish for a break before the halfway point. In the winter, with a storm blowing out of the south, it often became impassable. The wind tore across flat and mostly featureless expanse, gathering snow. A real gale could sweep that snow across the ground for miles, looking for a place to put it. Ditches and the borrow pits along roadsides were filled quickly and then burnished to an icy shine. Snowflakes changed as they tumbled across the land. They got pulverized, refined into uniform, minuscule crystals that rolled easily and packed densely together into something more like sand than snow.

The wind built strange things all over the ranch, but its masterwork was the enormous cornice at the top of the Stock Creek bench. In the dead of winter, with the right conditions, the cornice could take form overnight and stretch out for miles. It was massive, and arced so far out into space that it seemed to defy gravity. Chunks calved off and fell in piles on the slope below. Deep, dense snowdrifts grew at the foot of it. Such drifts lasted all through the winter and well into spring.

There must have come a moment, when the snow reached belly level and their legs began to bind, that the elk despaired of reaching the top. The wolves were just behind them, and the cornice towered overhead. The elk churned forward, postholing the deep, packed snow until they were high-centered and thoroughly mired. The wolves closed in behind them, walking lightly across the crust.

Under the Postcard Sky

*M*osquito season was in full swing by the beginning of July. Ahead of me on the trail, James's shirt was covered in gray bodies. The bugs moved across it slowly, stopping sometimes to probe through the cotton weave. I reached back and ran my hand along my horse's flank. Two passes covered my fingers in blood.

James, Jeremy, and I worked our way around a particularly remote portion of the ranch's southern boundary fence. We rode where we could, walked where we had to, and sometimes left the horses tied to stout trees while we fixed extremely bad sections. The valley was socked in with steely, bulge-bottomed clouds. It had drizzled all morning and started pouring at noon.

Rain was never warm on the Sun Ranch, but this shower felt particularly icy. A soaking rain, it set teeth chattering and numbed fingers into a state of complete uselessness. To walk in rain like that is bad. To ride through it is worse. I sat my horse and felt the warmth ebb from my feet and hands. When we hit breaks in the fence, I dismounted and tried to bend rusty wire to my will.

We sighted the fence's end as the first peals of thunder split the air and finished the final splices as bolts of lightning began crackling out of the southwest. They pounded the foothills on the far side of the Madison River for a while and then crossed it, sending us scuttling for shelter. We rode along an old logging road for a while, and then took cover in a grove of big Douglas firs beside Squaw Creek. We tied our horses, and James and I hunted for shreds of dry tinder while Jeremy worked with knife and lighter to make a fire in the wet dirt. He built a little smoldering pile and the three of us took turns blowing on it. I shivered until the fire caught, and then I steamed.

The smoke boiled up and knocked back the bugs. We stood by our blaze, in the midst of wild mountains and a godforsaken storm, and shared what little food we had, joking about neighboring ranches and discussing the progress of the grass. We talked the talk of hired men, about work that needed doing, the eccentricities of the owner, and short routes from one place to another. We told the secrets of the country, as if we could earn some title to the land by knowing it.

We let the fire die when the storm broke, and rode together toward the higher pastures and the barn. Every tree was dripping and the creeks had swollen. It occurred to me that I had achieved a rare thing: I was living at the center of my heart's geography. And I knew it.

———•◦•———

In July we moved cattle almost every day. More than any other chore on a ranch, herding is an art. When approached correctly, and if the animals are willing, a cattle drive becomes a complex, intriguing dance. I've always believed that cattle understand the steps a lot better than all but the most practiced and attentive humans. I won't claim to grasp the rules perfectly, but I've been around stock enough to know that their lives and movement are ruled by two interrelated principles: flight zone and herd instinct.

To understand the flight zone, imagine a rough circle around each cow in the herd. Certain animals—mostly other, familiar ruminants—are allowed inside the circle. The rest of the world's creatures, including cowboys, are personae non gratae.

Walk toward a bunch of contented, grazing cattle. At first they'll watch your progress with dull interest, as if you're in a sitcom they've seen before. Draw near the edge of the flight zone, however, and you'll quickly have their full attention. Heads jerk up into the air. Ears snap to attention. Worried glances fly back and forth within the herd.

Press the issue by taking another step or two forward, and the animal nearest you will react, generally by moving away. Working cattle in the open, grassy pastures above the Madison River, I learned to picture the flight zone as an elastic sphere, somewhat like a rubber kickball. When the sphere was pressed into from behind, the animal sprang away, forward. Direction mattered: pressure from the left rear would cause cattle to bend their course obliquely to the right, and pressure from the right would send them yawing to the left.

The process is not as simple as it sounds. The circle can vary infinitely in size based on the mood of the animal and the condition in which it finds itself. On the open range, when a herd is under constant harassment by predators or overzealous herders, the flight zone can expand all the way out to the horizon. In corrals, with the right sort of handling, it can diminish to a few feet. The animal's reaction once you're in the flight zone can vary, too: Yearlings often skip all the steps between curiosity and full-on panic. Older, more dominant cows will force you to prove that you're serious. They'll sometimes stand their ground until you're close, toss their heads, and paw the dirt to test your nerve. Make one wrong move with a cow like that, or hesitate for an extra, nervous beat, and she'll charge right over the top of you.

Misanthropic cows and human error aren't the only variables in herding. Terrain matters, too. The past experiences of the herd carry weight. The temperature and the barometer can make or break a day's work.

Nobody wants a stampede, humans or cattle. Controlled, sustained motion was our goal, so we tried to be judicious with the way we applied pressure. Generally, James, Jeremy, and I worked together to move herds, staying in an even line behind the animals, angling back and forth to nudge along any stragglers. The herding dogs, when James or Jeremy brought them, zipped back and forth along that line, filling any gaps between riders. Older, more experienced dogs understand the whole business perfectly. One of Jeremy's collies, Bonnie, had a particular talent for the work. She was calm and patient with most cattle and had an intense, focused stare that curbed bad behavior. Quick, vicious bites to the nose and hind legs—Bonnie's harshest punishments—were reserved for repeat offenders and egregious insubordination.

Younger dogs, like Jeremy's new pup or James's heeler, Tick, made more mistakes. When one of them pushed too hard or nipped the wrong hoof, agitation rippled like a wave through the heifers and steers.

When we wanted to turn our herds, we simply shifted our line—and the pressure we exerted—to one side or the other. If we did it right, the effect was striking: without anyone out in front to guide them, the cattle found a new trajectory. There always seemed to be something magical about the way they swung around like a compass needle finding north.

A cattle drive has to stay calm. It also has to be comprehensive—every member of the herd must arrive at the intended destination. Failing at this task even once or twice leaves stock scattered across the ranch, creates unnecessary work down the line, and gives the neighbors something to talk about. On a landscape as wild as the Sun Ranch, there were also spots in which leaving a heifer behind amounted to offering her up as a sacrifice.

Fortunately, the majority of the cattle despised being left as much as we hated to leave them. Their herd instinct runs deep, though not quite as strong as it does in elk or bison, which will tear apart the world to get back with their fellows. In cattle, the desire to stay close exerts a subtle but undeniable magnetism. Move one animal, and the cow alongside her will almost always follow. Trail a small bunch through a pasture of scattered, grazing yearlings, and a herd will fall in line and pile up like snow in front of a plow.

When everything was working well, it was possible to gently steer a herd across the land, ford creeks, pass in an orderly fashion through gates, and settle the cattle on new pasture with a minimum of stress. An outcome like that depended on a lot of things going right, some beyond our control and some within it. Above all else, success, safety, and the welfare of the cattle were contingent on our ability to remain calm and relaxed. When we lost our tempers, or tried to hurry, a wreck followed in short order.

———•·•———

One morning we were pushing cows down Highway 287 and wanted to have it done before nine, when tourists started heading for Yellowstone. It wasn't an especially big herd or a long move. The heifers gathered up easily enough and spilled through an open gate onto the asphalt. As the greenest of the crew, I rode behind the herd. Engulfed in the smell of fresh shit, I clattered my horse back and forth across the highway, pressuring stragglers. As I rode, I watched James work one of the roadside ditches and marveled at his knack with cattle. James knew precisely when to press ahead, and when to rein his horse. He stayed calm, and the animals in his care did the same.

Mostly, when the right-of-way fences were in good repair and nothing too exciting happened on either side of the road, we did well. The traffic was manageable: Locals waved and pushed their way through the herd. Tourists stopped, gawked, hung out their windows, and took photographs. I smiled for them. It thrilled me to be somebody's cowboy.

One Black Angus heifer in a herd of the same distinguished herself by turning and sprinting full tilt past me. She didn't look like much. I backtracked and double-timed her to the herd. She did it again. Cursing, I dropped to collect her. The second time, I chased at a hard lope and lodged her solidly in the middle of the bawling, jostling crowd. Her ear tag was blue, number 512.

Ahead, Jeremy had turned the leaders off the road and was counting the herd into their new pasture, moving his horse forward and back in the gate to keep their flow to a steady trickle. He ticked off numbers with his outstretched index finger.

Our heifers went through beautifully, with the exception of 512. Where the others turned left, she bolted right, crossing the highway and crashing headlong through a five-wire fence to take shelter in an overgrown willow thicket on the bank of the Madison River. When the rest of the herd was safely put away, we went after her.

At first 512 moved well, and I thought: Three riders, one animal—piece of cake. Getting her onto the highway was no problem, but as we neared the pasture gate, she veered, tore through the gap between James and me, and smashed her way back to the river.

For the next two hours we played cat and mouse with her, growing more frustrated with each failed attempt at getting her across the road. Finally, 512 snapped. Spraddle-legged and bug-eyed, she pawed, snorted, and rushed us, coming close enough to clip my stirrup leather.

We talked it over, and decided that she couldn't be left alone. The year before he came to the Sun, James had worked on another big cattle operation. Once, the owner of that ranch left a recalcitrant cow behind while moving his stock across the high-way. The rancher went home for dinner, leaving the cow to her own devices. Later, when the sirens of police cars and ambulances split the night, he knew that his cow had tired of solitude, crawled through the right-of-way fence, and tried to cross the blacktop in search of a way back to her herd. The resulting wreck took an unsuspecting driver's life, splattered the cow across fifty yards of pavement, and left the rancher brokenhearted.

Jeremy sent me trotting back to fetch the truck and horse trailer, so we could rope and load 512, haul her across the highway, and turn her loose with the rest of the herd. I bounced the rig out through the pasture, parked as close as I could, unloaded my horse, and climbed back into the saddle. James built a loop and threw it, catching 512 back of the neck. She spun and charged hard down the length of the rope, nearly catching him broadside. Jeremy got another rope around her neck, and the two of them began drag-ging her toward the trailer. She dug in with all four hooves. The horses strained, the ropes snapped tight, and she choked herself down. Wheezing, she tottered, buckled, and lay in the grass with her legs folded neatly beneath her.

I tried to shout her up. I spurred my horse against her but she would not move. James and Jeremy slacked their ropes and 512 gasped for air. She lay there regarding us, and for some reason she was infuriating. In spite of our wit, strategy, and perseverance, she was winning on sheer bulk and stubbornness. Her implacable resis-tance rendered us helpless. It shattered the image we held of our-selves as expert stockmen. Her posture said, I'll die right here, before you move me. Being new to the work, I did not know what to do.

James did, and as he tied off and dismounted, I saw a cold purpose in his eyes that knotted my stomach. He asked to borrow my lariat. I slid from the saddle, handed it over, and watched as he uncoiled four feet, starting from the knotted back end. With this, he delivered the most savage beating I had ever witnessed. Leaning back, James swung the knot in circles, fast enough to make it hiss. After three revolutions, he hunched down, striking the prostrate heifer about the eye and ear. Again. But 512 did not rise or bawl or move. She lay still and was beaten.

I don't know how long it lasted, only that it was long enough for me to wonder if James would ever stop. "Fuck it," Jeremy called down the rope. "We'll drag her."

Panting, James looked at me and said, "Get her up or she's dead."

He handed back my rope and walked to his horse. When James and Jeremy put their mounts forward, it was in unison and earnest. The ropes tightened and groaned against saddle leather. The heifer began to drag along with her neck stretched grotesquely and her eyes bulging. It was a moment before I remembered to kick her in the ass with all my strength. Nothing. I yelled and kicked again.

Miraculously, she stirred, struggled to her feet, and walked haltingly after the horses. She fell again. Violently, viciously, we got her up. It took another hour to load her, drive across the road, and cut her loose. Walking away, she was just a black shape between the high green grass of early summer and a postcard sky. It was easy to forget that she was bleeding.

———•◦•———

Not long after that day, James, Jeremy, and I woke early, caught our horses in the willow thickets along Moose Creek, and saddled in the barn. Jeremy walked over while I was checking the cinch on TJ and trying to decide whether or not to bring a slicker.

"Put this on," he said, and handed me a stained fishing vest. The vest had two big pockets, both of which were full of heavy, bulky items that clinked against each other as I worked the zipper.

"Try not to break those bottles. And watch out for the syringes, too. They sometimes come uncapped while you're riding."

Jeremy slid the barn door open and led his horse into the bright morning light. James and I followed him out through the pens to the road, where we checked our cinches and mounted. We trotted west, staying off the gravel for the sake of the horses' feet. I bounced along with a lariat slapping against my right leg and medicine bottles beating against my ribs.

We went through a wire gate and climbed to the top of the first small hill. Ahead of us, Orville's heifers were scattered like bits of salt and pepper across a panorama of grass and sage. Jeremy pulled out his notebook and read a handful of tag numbers. He described the heifers we were looking for and outlined his plan for the day. We'd ride the herd thoroughly, he said, beginning at the bottom of the pasture and working toward the top.

The pasture was shaped like a fat-ended banana. It enclosed a long, shallow draw that started at Badluck Way and then bent slightly north as it climbed toward the mountains. We rode in a rough line: I followed the north-side fence, James took the south side, and Jeremy zigzagged up the middle of the draw. I scanned each bunch of cattle carefully, and sometimes doubled back if one looked lame.

James found the first heifer. He eased her down the slope into the bottom, and then followed at a walk. Jeremy took down his rope, organized it in his hand, and began to build a loop. His practiced hands made the process look easy: Jeremy added two coils, flipping the loop each time he did to keep the line from twisting. The honda zipped down the rope until it sagged almost to the ground. Jeremy rode up alongside the heifer, swung through two slow circles, and dropped the rope lightly around her neck. He kept his horse even with the heifer, took up the slack, and dallied to his horn. Horse and cow moved in tandem for a while, and then Jeremy reined to a stop.

The rope snapped tight. The heifer wheezed against her noose and turned to face Jeremy. James swung his rope as she moved, laying a loop against her hind legs. When the heifer stepped through it, he jerked the slack. His horse braced against the rope, yanking both of the heifer's hind feet backward.

She teetered with her head stretched out grotesquely. Jeremy looked at me. "You pounce on her as soon as she falls."

The heifer groaned and toppled sideways. I slid off my horse, ran to her, and sank my knee into the side of her neck the way I had been told to. Then I reached out to grab her foreleg and folded it toward me.

"Good," Jeremy said. "She'll stay like that." He tied off, got down from his horse, and walked along the rope. The heifer struggled a couple of times as he approached, but I kept her pinned.

Jeremy unzipped one of the vest pockets and removed a bottle of liquid antibiotic and a massive syringe, which he filled to the "45 cc" mark. He tapped the plastic reservoir and shot a bit of medicine through the needle.

"Watch this part," he said. He took a fold of the heifer's neck skin between his fingers, slid the needle in, and injected a third of the medicine. Jeremy repeated the process in two other spots.

"This LA-200 is meant to be subcutaneous. Don't shoot it in a vein or you can mess the animal up. Try not to get it on your skin, either."

He pulled the needle out, wiped it clean, and rubbed the injection sites. I handed him a fluorescent-orange grease marker, and he used it to write the date in large numbers across the heifer's rib cage.

Jeremy walked back to his horse, mounted, and stepped forward so the neck rope went slack. Still holding the front leg, I reached forward and slid the loop off her head. I expected the heifer to move when I stood up, but she didn't. For an agonizing moment she lay dead still. I swung into my saddle and began to worry that we had treated her wrong. Too deep, I thought—Jeremy must have hit a vein. It was not until James took the pressure off his heel loop that she struggled up and took off running.

We rode uphill, repeating the vaccination drill as we came across more heifers and scouring the herd for signs of lameness and disease. Foot rot was the easiest, since a bad limp clued you in and a swollen, pus-spewing hoof confirmed the diagnosis. Pneumonia was harder to detect, because you had to look for general malaise. Number 512 emerged from a group of heifers, took one look at us, and loped off toward the pasture's far corner. Jeremy said she must have learned her lesson. I breathed easier knowing she was alive and well.

We doctored a handful of animals before reaching the top end of the pasture, all the ones on Jeremy's list and then some. One of the heifers was particularly hard to catch, probably because she had already seen the end of a few ropes. She knew how to dodge sideways at the last minute, and refused to run in a straight line. She kept far away from us and tried her utmost to stay in a tightly bunched herd.

Trying to catch her got dangerous in a hurry. Our slow, methodical operation went haywire and I found myself riding flat-out across a pasture riddled with badger holes, leaping sagebrush and old irrigation ditches, and trying hard to keep the heifer from turning. Working together, we took twenty minutes to wear her out. I stayed even with her hindquarters and tried to haze her toward ground that favored us. When my horse got tired, James took up the chase. He and Jeremy threw a dozen loops before they finally got her down.

I tried throwing a few heel shots that first day, but never caught anything. James and Jeremy did the roping, while I learned to pounce like a wildcat when the brisket hit the dirt. I practiced filling the needle, clearing it of air, and piercing through thick hide. It became second nature to drop knee-first on a thrashing heifer's neck, yank her front hoof back like a chicken wing, and get to work.

—•◦•—

As July ripened, each pasture move brought us closer to the mountains. The grass matured and we followed it into the high country, moving our animals from the lowest lands along the river to the flat, open benches at the center of the ranch, and finally on toward the rolling hills at the base of the Madison Range.

James and I preceded the herds. We checked fences, set out

salt and minerals in tubs made from old tires, and activated water lines and tanks that had lain dormant through the long months of winter. Crisscrossing the upper pastures, we rode four-wheelers in open country and we explored on horseback all the timbered nooks and crannies of Squaw Creek. When we passed bunches of cattle on our rounds, James showed me how to look for the most subtle signs of disease or lameness. From the way he studied a drooping ear or listless eye, James revealed how seriously he took the responsibility of keeping them from harm.

As we worked, we looked for wolves and found their sign with disconcerting regularity. One place, a pasture gate that wasn't far below the mouth of Bad Luck Canyon, nearly always held tracks and excrement in various stages of decay. Although wolf shit has a heinous stink and can carry a nasty parasite called *Echinococcus,* I always picked apart the fresher piles with a stick to make sure the hair inside belonged to elk instead of cattle.

Every day in early July led me on some type of great or little expedition. Each morning I set out with a long list of tasks that were scattered across the ranch: I might begin by setting out salt for the steers, roll east to check fence at the base of the mountains, swing north to fix a broken gate, then finish up by cleaning leaves and detritus from the spring box on Bad Luck Creek. On the way home, I would always loop back through some little hollow or drainage that I'd never seen before.

I made huge circles across the ranch, and surprised a great variety of animals with my presence. On the North End, small bunches of antelope broke and ran across the empty expanse of the Flats, trailing wisps of dust until they disappeared into some gentle swale or across the horizon. Deer leaped from grassy hides and took off running with the white flags of their tails held high. On more than a couple of tense occasions, I jumped moose in the willow thickets along the creeks. Their massive heads and dark, hulking shoulders were visible for a moment before receding into the brush. Hawks and eagles overflew my circumambulations. Jackrabbits tore pell-mell through the sage. Blue grouse burst from dark patches of timber, raising a racket loud enough to make my heart skip.

As I ranged higher and higher, I began to see more elk, both alive and dead. The vast herds of the early season had been scattered by the summer, strewn across the foothills below the Lee Metcalf Wilderness. A day rarely passed without my spooking a dozen or so of them from their day beds. They always headed for the high ground, and I watched group after group disappear into the mountains. I got the feeling that I was clearing the country of elk, displacing the natives to make room for our vast, bawling herds of steers and heifers.

From time to time I happened across a fresh elk kill or a wolf shit dead center in one of the wheel ruts. Though such things raised goose bumps, I tried not to dwell on them. I was, after all, the vanguard of a large and well-organized agricultural machine. We had fifteen hundred yearlings and a grazing plan to follow. I knew the pasture moves by heart: First, the heifers would graze the long, lush meadow just above the Big House. After a short week of that, we would move them uphill and over the Squaw Creek hogback, onto a grazing allotment we leased from the Forest Service.

No one doubted that the wolves were there and that they were hungry. As we forged ahead with our plans and expanded our range into the mountains, I grew increasingly aware that our margin for error was growing slimmer. We were staking new claims in the high parks and timber around Squaw Creek. Each elk carcass I discovered, and each bunch of them I sent scurrying for the peaks, further clarified the fact that we were falling into competition with the wolves for space and sustenance.

Even so, I thought that things would work themselves out. Our cattle would displace the elk, and we, with cracker shells, telemetry, and good intentions, would displace the wolves. We would be diligent. We would keep tabs. We would push the wild things into the higher reaches of the mountains, just for a few months. This was, after all, conservation ranching. After grabbing a little grass for our stock, we would get out, giving everything back to wild nature on the first of October.

The wolves were no longer hypothetical. Soon after we'd moved into the foothills, they chased elk through our fence and made a kill not far beyond the edge of a pasture. There, they could not have failed to see and smell the steers. When Jeremy worried aloud that they might return for a beef buffet, I started sleeping out with the cattle. It was a perfect job for me, really. James had his family. Jeremy had a girlfriend. Instead of going home alone, I kept company with the black outlines of mountains and innumerable stars.

The first night sleeping out, I was roused by a bawl that seemed surprised and a little scared. I went in search of the source, blundering through the dark with flashlight and shotgun at the ready, eventually finding that all was well. Since then I had learned to tell desperate, endangered bawls from more mundane communication within the herd. The cattle made strange and varied night noises; they moaned, bleated, and squealed.

One night I hopped in the truck and bounced up to join our herd in a brushy spot between the drainages of Moose and Bad Luck Creeks. After parking, I sat against the rear wheel to watch the day burn out. A fence line dominated the foreground, and hundreds of steers grazed beyond it, flecking the grass and sage with brown, white, and black.

The cattle quieted as the last light faded away. I made my bed behind the truck, setting pad and sleeping bag on the ground beneath the overhang of the flatbed. As I arranged my headlamp, bear spray, shotgun, and water bottle, I looked often at the dark ridgeline of the Moose Creek hogback. It served as the rampart between the domestic world and the wilderness beyond. I imagined the wolves running along there, looking down from that height at my white truck and bovine charges with something like contempt.

Perhaps I was projecting. More often than not, I viewed our steers as dumb and shitty creatures. Their noises seemed witless compared with the spine-tingling richness of a howl or the birdlike chirping of elk. As I zipped into my bag, I could not help thinking that, though I was paid to watch and protect the cattle, I wanted little to do with them. The wolves were what I had come for—to see and hear them, and maybe even keep them from getting into trouble. They, and not the bawling yearlings, had brought me into the foothills at night.

That sort of thinking felt like treason, especially on the eve of our push into the mountains. I stayed uneasy until the dead weight of exhaustion took hold.

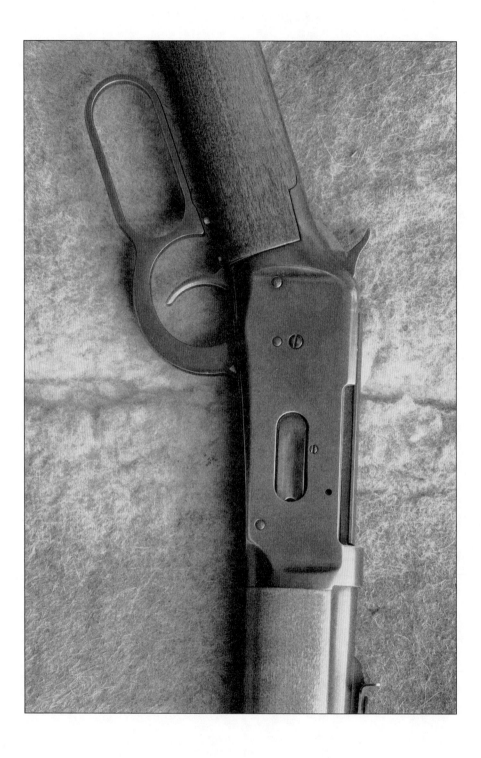

– III –

BONES

Predators

Working the Sun Ranch, I grew familiar with animal death in all its forms. Moving through the drainages of Bad Luck, Moose, and Squaw Creeks during the height of summer meant navigating a landscape of carcasses. In time, I learned to identify different carnivores from their handiwork and tried to reconstruct the particulars of hunts from the meager evidence of skeletons.

The grizzly, for instance, was a powerful glutton. Once, while tasked with looking for straggler cattle after a pasture move, James and I rode our horses along one of the faint paths that threaded through the timber in the

Moose Creek bottom. Down there I caught the unmistakable reek of death, mixed with some muskier, choking odor. For the better part of half an hour, we looked fruitlessly for a carcass. As we searched, James's dogs grew nervous. They began to bark—not their usual yips, but low, fearful, rasping sounds. My horse began to snort and tighten underneath the saddle. When we found a steer's skin behind a tree, shucked off whole and crumpled like a candy wrapper, the hair on the back of my neck stood up.

Bears aren't picky, and since they don't turn their noses up at a rotting carcass, we couldn't be sure about the steer's cause of death. Bears are, however, extremely possessive of the kills to which they lay claim. As James kept a close watch on the timber around us, I slid off my horse and cut the tag from the steer's ear. We beat a hasty retreat out of the trees.

Up in the meadow we made it to the top of a little hill in time to see a sow griz and her two cubs charge out of the creek bottom and make a run for the peaks. They moved at a shambling lope that made surprisingly short work of big country. From a distance, they looked strangely human as they climbed across a barbwire fence. We hadn't caught them in the act of killing cattle, so we let them go.

A mountain lion is the bear's antipode. A grizzly survives by brute force. In contrast, a cat gets by on stealth. During one week in July, I found several lion kills in the Moose Creek canyon. Each deer had been dragged to a suitably private spot, partially eaten, and then covered up with dirt. The violence seemed to go on mostly at night. Though I watched carefully as I drove the road at dusk and dawn, I did not catch sight of the creature responsible.

I saw a lion just once during my time on the Sun. It was early morning, before sunrise, and I had trekked through the darkness to stake out a wolf den, hoping to catch a glimpse of newborn pups. As I hid in the grass with a pair of binoculars, waiting for the wolves to emerge, a group of elk crossed the steep face of a foothill far above the den. Without them, I never would have seen the cat.

A cow elk looked uphill toward some timber, and then stiffened as if a jolt of current had run her through. I followed her stare to the tree line and watched the lion emerge. Through my binoculars, he was huge, tawny, and unbelievably muscular. His forearms were massive, bigger in proportion to the rest of him than the limbs of wolves, bears, or anything else I knew of on the ranch. Though he loomed large in my binoculars, the lion virtually disappeared against a backdrop of dry grass and sage. A thick, bushy tail arced out behind him, occasionally switching languidly from side to side. He seemed to be in total control, and in no particular hurry.

The lion moved carefully. He did not trot, or even really walk. He lifted one foot at a time, swung it forward, and set it gently in the grass. After every movement, he stopped and waited. Even from a distance I could tell that he was trying to be quiet as he advanced slowly toward an outcropping of rock above the elk.

I don't think the elk could see him, because the slope of the hillside leveled off above the herd, hiding the cat from view. Still, the cow had sensed that he was there. Perhaps the swirling wind betrayed him or some twigs snapped underfoot. Whatever it was, the herd became agitated, bunched together, and swung around toward the hidden tom, like weather vanes in a hard breeze.

A strange thing happened then: instead of breaking and running downhill, the lead cow charged, pounding uphill toward the lion. A few of her herd mates followed. With her nose in the air and cows at her back, she closed the distance until she stood thirty paces from the big cat.

A tense standoff ensued. Well and truly busted, the lion stood up tall and looked straight at the elk. For an agonizing moment, the lead cow seemed unsure about what to do next. Then she took a defiant step forward. The lion stepped back. Another, and he spun on his heels, took two bounds, and melted into the trees. The elk watched and waited for a while, then turned and headed slowly south.

Bears have strength. Cats have patience. A wolf has endurance and a family. On paper, in comparison with a goliath like the grizzly or a specialist like the cougar, a wolf seems small, ill equipped, and inconsequential. They have teeth, sure, but no real claws to speak of. To see one standing knee-high to an elk is to wonder how they ever manage to get the job done.

In practice, however, wolves did most of the killing on the ranch. They were successful on the North End Flats, in the confines of Bad Luck Canyon, and in the strange, dark bogs along Squaw Creek. Wherever they found prey, the wolves figured out a way to take it down.

Wolves make their living by traveling far and working together. During winter, on the north end of Yellowstone Park, in the frozen expanse of the Lamar Valley, I watched a group of wolves hunt elk.

It was a large pack, twelve or thirteen adults, and they managed to split two cows off from the rest of the herd. Seeing them run prey to exhaustion was thrilling and terrifying. The wolves were relentless, churning through six inches of fresh powder and taking turns pushing the pace. The chase ranged across a few good-sized hills and went so far that I had to drive down the road to keep up with it. The way they hazed and tired the cows reminded me of how James, Jeremy, and I worked together to rope and doctor cattle.

Toward the end, the elk were knackered. One cow fell behind the other as they started up a final hill, and the pack took notice. A wolf took a leap at her flank and missed. Another took a crack at it, and briefly got its teeth into meat.

The first moments of that kill were almost playful and looked similar to the way cattle dogs hustle along a lazy steer. The wolves nipped at the elk's heels, and she responded by putting on one last burst of speed. After that, things turned serious. A wolf bit the cow high on her hindquarter and hung on for a few steps. The elk stumbled as she shook him off, missing a beat in the high-stakes dance of running.

Her momentary lapse gave the wolves an advantage and they pressed it. Another member of the pack sank his teeth in and held on. A third edged up alongside, reached high, and bit her hard near the base of the neck. The cow crumpled under the weight, pitching forward in the snow. Her hooves came thrashing up for a second, and then the pack was on her. They crowded in, wagging tails and shoving each other around. Though I couldn't see everything, it was clear that her legs were still kicking weakly when they started to part her out.

The other cow, exhausted, made it to the top of the hill and stopped in a small cluster of scattered pines. The trees were old giants, and their widespread branches had preserved a circle of bare, snowless ground around each massive trunk. The surviving elk stopped in one such circle, no more than two hundred yards from where the wolves were feasting, and she waited.

After perhaps fifteen minutes, a pair of wolves left the bloody mess of the kill to follow her tracks uphill. They trotted into the pine grove and stopped in front of her. The elk pressed her rump against the trunk of the tree and refused to move.

The standoff lasted for the better part of an hour. Frequently, one of the wolves edged in toward the big pine. When it crossed from snow onto bare ground, the elk charged forward. She held her nose in the air and struck at the wolf with both front hooves. As soon as the wolf turned tail, the cow walked back to her tree and stood against the trunk.

Just as they had worked together in the chase, the wolves took turns harassing the surviving cow elk. Members of the pack trickled steadily back and forth between the site of the kill and the spot where the elk had chosen to make her stand. Once in the pine grove, however, the wolves seemed less than serious. Some lay full-bellied in the snow and simply watched her with interest. A few tried halfheartedly to bait her away from the pine.

The elk stuck to her guns. When the wolves got too close she lashed out at them. Otherwise, she simply sidestepped around the tree. Always, she was careful to keep the nearest wolves in sight and her vulnerable hind end safely pressed against bark.

In the end, the wolves gave up and left her in the grove. They paused awhile by their kill to chase scavenger birds off the remnants and eventually headed uphill and out of sight. The elk stayed put for a while, and then she walked away.

On the Sun Ranch, as in Yellowstone, a wolf kill was immediately, conclusively identifiable. If fresh, it retained the aspect of a violent feeding frenzy. I found the remnants of one dead elk that could not have been more than a few hours old. First I saw the blood, a thick trail daubed across the tops of sagebrush and bunchgrass, ending at a scene of messy dismemberment. Around the carcass, the grass was matted down and slicked with blood and half-digested grass from the rumen. Scattered tufts of hair formed a great, uneven halo. Inside that ring, a five-hundred-pound cow elk had been efficiently reduced to a pile of parts. The meat was about half gone and at its thickest had yet to completely cool. When I lifted up one of the shredded back legs, drops of blood ran down to the ground below. The other hindquarter was gone, snapped off red and clean at the femur. Most of the ribs had been cracked into fibrous, shattered messes. In the grass around the carcass were leftover bits from the organs and entrails, including a pink, frothy, fist-sized chunk of lung.

Perhaps the strangest, most disturbing part of the scene was that, in the midst of all that carnage and blood, I could not help thinking that the meat looked good enough to eat. Big chunks of it remained on the carcass, and it would have been no great trouble to pull out my pocketknife, trim away the tooth marks, and cut myself a thick steak.

But something stopped me from unfolding the blade. I grew uneasy and began to look hard at the land around me. It wasn't that I expected the wolves to emerge, though I knew they weren't finished with the carcass. It wasn't that I doubted the quality or cleanliness of the meat. In fact, I had long been waiting to try some elk. The ranch was dotted with headless, knife-gouged skeletons left over from past hunting seasons, and everyone I talked to seemed ready to corroborate the fact that elk agreed incredibly well with the human palate.

I wanted the meat but felt a deep, vague sense of revulsion. I was not, I thought, a predator—at least not like the wolves. Sure, I ate meat, but I did not tear life apart at the seams and swallow its guts before the heart stopped beating. I was different, I told myself—a gentler creature. I kept my knife in my pocket, left the kill to the wolves, and turned my attention back to the care and feeding of cattle.

Late one afternoon, a silver car drove up Badluck Way, a flashing speck that cruised out of the Moose Creek canyon and headed up the road toward the Big House. I leaned against a stock tank and watched it move across the land. I didn't know anyone who owned a silver car, and James and Jeremy were in town.

No public road crossed the Sun Ranch. With the exception of Badluck Way, all the ranch roads that reached the highway were gated. In spite of the No Trespassing signs that hung from our perimeter fences, occasional strangers still wandered onto the ranch.

I was nervous the first time I stopped a car. Jeremy told stories about poachers and midnight chases across rough country. He kept a pistol in the glove compartment. All I had were fencing pliers and the distinct sense that something would go wrong. What do I say? I wondered. What if they tell me to go to hell?

The vast majority of people turned out to be lost tourists. The ones who knew they were trespassing acted guilty and nervous, usually apologizing before I could say hello and heading straight off the place when I asked them to. I got comfortable with such dirt-road conversations, and even came to like them.

When the silver car appeared, chasing it down seemed like a welcome break from work. I put the four-wheeler in gear and gunned it down a two-track. At Badluck Way I spun my hat around so it faced backward and opened the throttle. Twenty, thirty, forty, fifty miles per hour. The engine roared.

I closed in on the car, letting off the gas when the dust started to make me cough. The driver must have seen me, but he didn't pull over. He rolled down the road, passed the shop, and pulled into the driveway at the Big House. I stopped behind him.

The car was a big Audi sedan, an A8. It was brand-new and immaculate except for the dust from driving up the road. A Wyoming vanity plate hung on the bumper: SPUR.

A tall, gray-haired man climbed out and blinked in the sun. He said his name was George and stuck out his hand. He didn't seem lost, guilty, or nervous.

We talked about the heat, the view—nothing. I waited for him to explain himself, to justify his presence here on the ranch, but he didn't. When our conversation lagged, I asked him straight out:

"What brings you up to the ranch today?"

I was being nice. Usually I would have said, "Do you know you're on private property?"

He gave me one of those you-don't-know-who-you're-dealing-with smiles and told me Roger had sent him up to have a look at the view from the Big House.

"You work for Roger, then?" I asked.

"Not exactly." George chuckled. "I'm a consultant."

We shot the breeze for a few more minutes. George talked a lot but didn't say much about his purpose. When he headed back down the road and left me standing in the Big House driveway, I knew only that he had worked for thirty years in Jackson Hole, planning the layouts of resorts and high-end developments.

This worried me and brought to mind a conversation I'd had with Roger not long before on Badluck Way. I was headed home for the evening, and the sun had almost settled on the Gravelly Range when Roger flagged me down. After I rolled the big white work truck to a stop and he wiped the dust from his black cover-all sunglasses, Roger asked a few questions about the movements of the heifer herd, the last known location of the wolf pack, and other ranch minutiae. He seemed eager to talk, so I shut off the engine, stepped out of the cab, and stood in the road.

Roger, surprisingly, wanted to know about me. He asked about my background and my reason for coming to the Sun. I told him my story in a nutshell—that I had come to the ranch because I liked the work and loved the land. I enjoyed being alongside the wilderness and making my living from it.

He gave a slight nod in the affirmative.

"What are you going to do when the grazing season's over?"

The question wasn't new to me. In my rare quiet moments, after dinner in the bunkhouse, or in between daytime tasks, I often wondered where the coming winter would find me. There were plenty of options, ranging from embarking on a career as a lifelong cowboy to applying to the University of Montana to get a master's degree in something useful. Standing on Badluck Way, I tried to keep things simple.

"I want to stay out here," I told Roger. "Do something that keeps this place wild, open, and undeveloped."

I launched into a vicious little tirade about subdivisions, specifically the one that huddled against the foothills of the Madison Range just across the ranch's north boundary. Ranchettes I said, were blights on the landscape, perversions of the Western dream.

"Sure," Roger replied, "but you've got to be reasonable about it. Agriculture doesn't pay the bills on a place like this. I don't see how it could, which means the whole thing's unsustainable on some level."

He went on to say that the ranch was deep in debt and that the profits from our summer grazing barely balanced the cost of hiring help, servicing equipment, and keeping the buildings standing. It fell short of the land payment by a couple of important decimal places.

Roger explained that he believed a truly sustainable ranch could be built on a tricornered foundation. The first main enterprise was ranching—often of the seasonal type that we engaged in on the Sun. The second leg was a combination of tourism and recreation—hunting, fishing, and all the other earthly pleasures offered down at Papoose Creek. The last part of the equation was limited, responsible real estate development.

"Nobody likes it," he said. "Least of all me. But look at the math. A place like this can't survive by breaking even on cows. Elk hunters aren't going to pay the mortgage, either, no matter how much we charge them."

A homesite on the Sun would sell for a few million, easy, especially if it came with hunting rights, access to the rest of the property, and privileges at a lodge like Papoose Creek. Sell a handful of them, and the ranch would be out of the red in a hurry.

He stopped there and looked away to the west. The sun was gone, but the sky still burned orange above the Gravellies, and the scattered clouds were lit from beneath with a white light so intense it made me squint.

Roger pulled off and folded his sunglasses. When he looked back toward me, no trace remained of his customary smile. Without its usual shield, Roger's face looked grim and exhausted.

"Hell of a place," he said.

"That it is."

He wished me a good evening and drove off toward the Big House. When his car had passed from sight, I climbed onto the truck's flatbed and leaned against the headache rack to watch the day end. I had a hard time arguing with Roger's logic. Ranching didn't pay, and a couple more houses might not make much difference in the grand scheme.

Still, I hated picturing the office, somewhere in Ennis or Virginia City, where a filing cabinet held a map of lower Squaw Creek crisscrossed with property lines, utilities, and new roads. Building a house in the wilderness was easy. It took paperwork, lumber, and a few other details. On the outskirts of Twin Bridges, Whitehall, Sheridan, and a dozen other nearby towns, an army of contractors waited to be unleashed. One phone call and a little pile of money, and the deal would be done.

After the consultant left, I looked southeast and saw the moon rising, nearly full, above the Madison Range. Somewhere out there the wolves were waking up, stretching out, and getting ready. The elk were moving, too, along with countless other creatures. As I pictured them all traveling by moonlight, unwatched and largely unbothered, a cold dread settled like anesthesia in my stomach.

———•·•———

We had an old radio receiver, a leftover from the summer when a pair of graduate students had stayed on the ranch to track the movements of elk and wolves. The receiver looked like a chubby version of the radios we carried to communicate with each other, except it had a cord at one end that connected to a collapsible metal antenna.

An hour before sunset I stood on a hill, switched on the unit, and held out the antenna like a dowsing rod. I faced the mountains and turned slowly through the points of the compass. With the receiver pressed against my ear I listened to the hiss of static. I turned the volume up and swept the horizon until a faint click came out of the speaker, indicating that one of the collared wolves was within a few miles.

The noise was slow, and regular as a metronome. It began when I pointed the antenna at Bad Luck Canyon, increased in volume as I swept south, and then died away at the end of the Moose Creek hogback. I dialed down the gain until the clicking stopped and flipped the antenna perpendicular to the ground. I swept again, narrowing the scope of my search. I repeated the process, decreasing the gain and volume until the noise was confined to a small slice of the Madison Range. Sighting down the antenna, I decided that the wolf we called Rotten Teeth had stopped to rest in a little draw just north of Moose Creek.

Rotten Teeth was old—the lupine equivalent of a septuagenarian. He often left the pack and wandered solo. In the pictures taken when the Fish, Wildlife & Parks guys collared him, his mouth was an awful mess of decay and blunt stumps. According to the biologists, the smell was awful. Mostly wolf teeth look like the sheer scarps of the Madisons, but Rotten Teeth's dentition brought to mind the worn, smooth nubs of the Gravelly Range. Given the condition of his jaws, it seemed a miracle that he stayed alive.

Setting down the antenna, I punched a new radio frequency into the receiver and began to search for another member of the pack. I swept the eastern skyline with the gain and volume high. Rotating in a full circle, I heard nothing but the usual electronic hiss and roar. When I turned south toward Squaw Creek, I thought I heard a single faint click but couldn't be sure. Holding the antenna still, I listened for another. Nothing came.

The problem with tracking wolves is that they do their most interesting business at night and live in a complex, mobile, and fluid society. From day to day, it is impossible to be sure which wolves are running together, which are off on some private errand, and which might have left the pack altogether to try their luck in other drainages. All I knew for sure was that the Wedge Pack lived higher than I did on the mountain, often rousted out at sunset, and crossed the landscape seemingly without effort.

We had two collars in the pack and wanted more. Since the signals were easily interrupted by topography, and much of the ranch consisted of steep hills, keeping tabs on the pack was difficult. With a feature like the Moose Creek hogback breaking the connection between transmitter and receiver, it was possible to be quite close to the wolves without ever picking them up.

Mostly we heard nothing on the receiver. One strong signal was a notable event, and two constituted a red-letter day. Mike, the valley's Fish, Wildlife & Parks wolf biologist, took a similar view. To him, more collars meant more information and a better account of how the Wedge Pack used the land. During the long days of mid-July, Mike visited the ranch more frequently, aiming his receiver at the mountains, hypothesizing about the location of den sites, and finally setting a toothless leghold trap in hopes of laying hands on a new wolf.

Unable to locate a wolf, I shut off the receiver, folded the tines of the antenna, and strapped it to the rack on the four-wheeler. A dirt road took me to the top of the square-mile pasture where our stock was settled. The sun was low enough to set the bunchgrass glowing, and the grazing cattle looked like shadows. I parked, shut off the engine, and began to walk along the pasture's upper end.

Two kinds of fence surrounded our cattle. The inner fence was permanent and made of barbwire, the outer one was the temporary construction called fladry, a technology which we'd borrowed from European shepherds. Tired of losing animals to predation, they had designed a movable barrier intended to keep wolves away from their herds. The fladry we used was just a string of bright-red plastic flags set a foot apart and hung so that their free ends brushed the ground. Small fiberglass posts, the same sort we used for temporary electric fence, supported the line. Since the wind blew almost all the time, the flags stayed in constant, chaotic motion. They flapped, flailed through the grass, and slapped against each other. This was supposed to scare the wolves.

Now that I had seen what wolves could do to elk, I was as skeptical that flags could stop them as the rancher who'd offered me her rifle. The wolves were smart and ravenous, but I figured that any sort of deterrent was better than none at all. As the crow flies or the wolf trots, the cattle were no more than a mile and a half from Rotten Teeth. For an animal that maintains a territory of more than a hundred square miles and lopes up mountains without any signs of visible effort, a mile and a half is inconsequential.

I walked along the fladry, untangling flags that the wind had knotted and adjusting the tension of the line. The sun had set by the time I got back to the four-wheeler. As I rolled out my sleeping pad, the wolves began to howl.

The sound is arresting, strange, and beautiful. Biologists offer detailed, clinical descriptions of the howl—its frequency, amplitude, and variability—coupled with impressive accounts of how the pack reacts once the first wolf lets loose. Yet even the experts wonder what howling means to the animals that do it. Howling has been construed as a summons to the members of the pack, a call meant to draw far-flung animals together. It's also thought to be a challenge to other wolves, an aggressive advertisement of a pack's ownership of the landscape. Howling has been characterized as a celebration of the hunt, an expression of pure, unadulterated joy, and half a dozen less plausible things.

I suspect there's no simple answer to what howling means to the wolves. I've heard them sound eager, hopeful, and confident, like athletes running through a pregame chant. I have awakened in the night to a single, mournful voice from the dark and wondered at how it managed to transcend the bounds of species and language to leave me wide-eyed and heartsore.

With my back against the wheel, I listened to the ascending

notes of that foreign language for what seemed like a long time. The howling stopped as abruptly as it started, leaving only the hiss of wind-jostled grass and the rhythmic crunch of grazing. I settled down to sleep between the wolves and the cattle, under a bright moon and a clear black sky.

The pups grew quickly. As spring became summer they ceased to be a mass of writhing, squalling fur balls and learned to run. They left the den, following the other members of the Wedge Pack up Bad Luck and over the stony divide that looks out toward Hilgard Peak and the ranch's South End. The pups trotted along, poking at old bones and learning the paths on which they would soon have to make a living. They waited at rendezvous sites—hidden places in the thick timber and deep ravines along the edge of the Lee Metcalf Wilderness—while the rest of the pack hunted.

When the wolves returned, the pups mobbed them for food. They pressed in close, whining and licking at muzzles until the hoped-for, half-digested wads of meat and gristle came up. The pups consumed everything ravenously and fought each other for the largest scraps. As they ate, they got stronger. Big canines, carnassials, and molars pushed out their milk teeth, and the pups sprouted long, thin marathoners' legs. They soon put those legs to use following their elders on great, looping circumnavigations of the Wedge Pack's territory.

The pack numbered nine without the pups. Including them brought the total to thirteen animals—thirteen mouths to feed. For a bunch like that, a white-tailed deer amounted to an appetizer and an elk carcass didn't last long.

In winter, when snow had kept the vast herds of elk bunched together in the low country, getting their fill had been simple enough. When the elk dropped their spotted calves in early June, *it was downright easy.* As July passed, however, things began to change. With their calves bulked up on milk and green grass, the elk began their annual migration to the high country. In groups of a few, a dozen, or a hundred, they made the arduous climb up Moose Creek to Finger Lake, then on through the boulders of Expedition Pass. Once they crossed into the Gallatin drainage, the herds broke up and vanished into the thick forests and innumerable alpine valleys of the Lee Metcalf Wilderness.

The older wolves knew what hard hunting waited for them up there. In the high mountains, with lush grass everywhere and no snow to restrict their movements, the elk were nearly impossible to find and kill. The wolves remembered ranging far and going hungry, and they stayed in the foothills as long as the food held out. It worked for a while. Late elk calves and stragglers died by the dozen, but soon the pack had thoroughly gleaned the North End.

So they hunted south, down past Moose Meadows. They still visited the northern part of their territory, traveling frequently across the face of the Pyramid, through Badluck, out into the Mounds and beyond. They made occasional kills there, but the vast expanses of the North End were a shadow of what they had been—largely barren of elk and too full of the sight and sound of man.

In the steep hills and dense thickets of Squaw Creek, however, summer came later, the elk stayed longer, and humans rarely ventured in, sticking to a very few roads and trails when they did come. In Squaw Creek, the Wedge Pack found its summer home.

The wolves slept through the hot hours in day beds along the creek, hidden from the world by a warren of fallen timber and treacherous boggy ground. At dusk they rousted out, howled themselves ready, and ran elk by moonlight.

They did well, but must have felt their fat days were numbered. Every morning, more elk departed for the mountains. Every night, the wolves had to work a little harder, run a little farther for their food. Men from the ranch came more frequently to Squaw Creek, checking fence and leaving their sign and scent in the heart of the Wedge Pack's territory. As July wore on, the wolves could not have failed to notice that the season was changing.

Leaving the Road Behind

*O*n the hunt for a handful of missing cattle in high summer, I ended up on the South Fork of Squaw Creek, which must have been the greenest, most overgrown place in all Montana. The standing trees grew close together, and downed ones lay like pick-up sticks, and everything was covered with layers of spongy moss. I rode carefully along a game trail with my horse stepping over logs high enough to graze his belly, passing moldering, scattered bones.

I can't say for sure how I lost my way—it felt as though the trail deserted me, as if it quailed and fled from under the hooves of my horse. It was just gone and I was left playing Twister with fallen timber on a hummock between two little streams of water.

The horse was afraid. He would go no farther and balked at turning back. The bog or something in it paralyzed him. When I forced him across one of the streams, the ground gave way and sank him to the girth. There was no warning, just a sucking sound and then my boots were on the ground. I dismounted and crawled out with my horse plunging wildly behind me. I judged the place to be worse than Bad Luck Canyon and could not shake the sense that something watched my struggles with hungry interest.

That was the way of things in summer. Every place, it seemed, belonged either to the ranch crew or the wolves. As a rule the open, grassy places were ours. Dark, overgrown spots like Squaw Creek belonged to the Wedge Pack.

The boundaries were far from settled. They changed with the weather and every time day gave way to night. Both the crew and the pack crossed often into each other's domains. When darkness fell, the wolves trotted through our pastures with impunity. They pissed on gateposts and killed elk in disconcerting proximity to the cattle herds.

We made more extensive forays into the wildest parts of the ranch. James and I checked miles of fence, looked for lost cattle in places that hadn't seen a human in years, and rode scouting trips in hopes of finding rendezvous sites used by the pack and better understanding the way the wolves moved through the foothills. We pushed farther and farther into the heart of their summer hunting grounds, taking our livestock with us into the high country.

The tension between the ranch crew and the Wedge Pack had wrought a change in me. That summer I began to look differently at the land. I peered harder into the shadowed depths of the forest, rose earlier, and stayed outdoors longer in the evenings. Because of this I saw more animals than I had before—deer, antelope, elk, coyotes, bears, badgers, and wolves.

I changed my routes across the landscape. As a runner, I always went out jogging after work. Even on long days, exhausting ones that started early and ended with the setting sun, I swapped jeans for shorts, cowboy boots for running shoes, and took off across some chunk of the ranch.

When I first arrived on the Sun, I kept mostly to the gravel roads. In July, as we began to push more seriously against the wolves, I switched quickly from gravel to dirt tracks. In short order, I left the ruts in favor of game trails.

Every night, at or after sunset, I ran the benches and hills of the Sun Ranch. I'll admit that I was looking for trouble. When I saw deer or elk from a long way off, I tried to sneak up on them. Using the features of the land—little bumps and hollows I had never noticed before—I did my best to get close.

It was wicked, feral fun. I drew near herds of deer, elk, and antelope, sometimes crawling on my hands and knees to stay hidden in the sage and grass. When the animals saw or smelled me, I sprinted toward them, scattering them to the horizon. They always left me in the dust, alone and smiling under a many-colored sky.

I chased everything I could—coyotes, jackrabbits, and a badger who unexpectedly turned to fight. Once, in a moment of extremely poor judgment, I ran a black bear up Moose Creek and
then looked over my shoulder all the way back down. There was
never malice in it, only simple joy. I loved to feel the wind, lay
claim to my landscape by crossing it, and watch the deer outpace
me before disappearing in the rising night.

———•◦•———

On a weekday afternoon I volunteered to go with Mike, the Fish,
Wildlife & Parks biologist, to check his traps. We soon found a
wolf lunging back and forth in a little gap in the sagebrush. From
where we crouched at the crest of a small hill, we could not see the
trap that held it, but knew it was there because of how the wolf
rose, sprinted three steps, and then flipped grotesquely when the
chain snapped tight.

Mike dropped onto all fours and crawled through the brush. He
carried a jab stick at the ready, and small bottles of dope clinked in
the pockets of his backpack. I followed, holding a noose pole in my
left hand and smelling the familiar tang of crushed sage. Mike de-
toured around the bigger plants, breaking twigs and dirtying his
crisp, tan uniform. We worked our way down the hill, kneeling at
intervals to raise our heads like periscopes.

"Yearling," Mike said. "Male." He knew it from a glimpse and
assessed the wolf confidently, the way I would pick a heifer from
our herd of steers.

The wolf surged back and forth. Sometimes he rolled clear
over the caught foreleg, thumping to the ground and staying out
of sight for a handful of gut-wrenching seconds. Otherwise he

stretched his limb out so that it pointed at where the brush hook tangled in the sage. He stood against the chain and yanked until it seemed his foot would tear away. The bush shook and recoiled, as if the wolf were strong enough to uproot it.

"What if he pulls loose?"

Mike answered in a low voice, from the side of his mouth: "He'll just hook to the next one. Probably did a couple times already."

The bush held. The wolf glared down his leg and the arc of the chain. He panted, then charged forward, leaped the anchor shrub, spun at the end of the chain, and dropped out of sight.

As we sneaked nearer, I forced myself to get lower. With my face six inches from the ground, I passed over elk shit, old bone shards, and jackrabbit runs, following Mike's boot soles. Mike was not raising his head anymore, and I began to worry that we were covering ground too quickly and would soon round a bush and come face to jaws with the wolf. I took some comfort in the fact that Mike would have to greet him before I did.

When Mike did stop to take another look, we were twenty yards away from the yearling. He motioned me behind him and spoke across his shoulder:

"Let's wait and see if he gets calm enough to noose."

The wolf looked our way and made a noise that was not quite a howl or a growl, but held the most menacing features of both. Mike sat back on his heels. "Watch him."

The wolf stared at Mike, bared his teeth, and rushed us. When the chain caught, it jerked the forepaw back below the wolf's deep chest. The wolf did not yelp or move to slack the pressure of the chain, but faced us steadily on three legs, looking strangely like a pointer dog hot on a scent. After holding the pose for a moment, he broke and ran obliquely away from us until the chain downed him again.

"Aggressive—we'll have to dart him," he said. "The gun is in the truck."

The wolf raised his muzzle and let go a deep, quavering moan. Mike slung his backpack around and pulled a camera from the main pocket.

"I'll get it. Could you take some pictures?"

He held out the camera and I took it, hardly feeling the weight. Mike left, taking the noose and jab stick with him. The truck was a solid quarter mile away—a round-trip of ten minutes at the very least. I knelt in the sage and wondered what to do.

At first I tried to avert my gaze, aiming it at a chunk of ground a little ways to the left of the wolf, but my stare wouldn't stay put. It wandered to the tine of the brush hook and up the nestled links of the chain to the spot where dark metal and silver fur met in a shining mess of blood.

The trap was a Newhouse, similar to the ones used during the extermination campaigns that had cleared this country of wolves in earlier times. There were, however, some notable differences: The trap was rigged with a transmitter that sent a specific signal when the jaws were sprung. This had let Mike arrive quickly on the scene, minimizing the amount of time that the wolf had to spend in agony. The trap was also toothless, its jaws made of smooth steel. The principle behind it was similar to that of fishing with a barbless hook. A smooth trap might lose a wolf more often, but it was easier on the bones and tissues of the foot, at least in theory.

Steel and flesh seldom play well together, however, and the wolf's paw looked as though it had been beaten with a hammer. The jaws had clearly worked their way through the skin, and they pressed together so tightly that I had trouble believing that bones and ligamenture could remain whole between them. Below the trap his toes splayed out unnaturally, like a specimen readied for necropsy.

The wolf stood in a clearing of his own making, surrounded by broken chunks of sagebrush, a few daubed with red. He held his caught foot off the ground and panted as if his chest would burst. All this, I thought, to get a radio collar on him? All this gory business to point an antenna at the mountains and hear a click?

I looked higher, and then the full force of his stare caught me. His eyes were pale, though their precise color escapes me. They were green, yellow, and blue at once, rimmed around with delicate black lines striking off from the outer corners toward the ears. His eyes did not waver. He never averted them and I did not see him blink. There was something irresistible and sapping about the wolf's stare, like water moving against a loose-soil bank. His eyes cut into my foundation. I was about to fall forward. I couldn't move. I looked away.

When I dropped my gaze he sat up straight and howled until the mountain broke open in reply. At first the response was like an echo or the usual round whistle of the wind, but within moments, I knew his pack had answered. Their combined voice came tumbling from the high country, rolling like water down the draws. Distinct notes and the sounds of pups yipping in accompaniment blended into a strange, ululating mass of sound that filled the world. This chorus was wholly different from the noise they made before a night hunt. Hearing it made my hair stand and my heart sink. The wolves were keening, trying to call back one of their own that man and daylight had put beyond reach. I worried that the pack was watching, and that they would follow their voices down the mountain.

The wolf went quiet. He sat very straight and devoured the haunting sounds the way a death row inmate must eat his last meal. When the howling died away, he did not answer it or fight the chain.

The wolf kept still and watched me. Something had been decided and it had dimmed his gaze. Now I could look without completely losing my moorings. I remembered the camera, raised it up, and, feeling like a tourist at a messy highway wreck, snapped frames without focusing.

Mike returned, and we moved quickly. I walked around one side of the wolf, distracting him, while Mike thumped him in the flank with a tranquilizer dart full of ketamine and xylazine. We backed off and waited until the drugs took hold. The wolf began to weave unsteadily from side to side and then dropped suddenly, in a heap.

Mike approached him slowly, touched the wolf gently with the barrel of the tranquilizer gun, then knelt and slipped the trap from his leg. With the metal gone I could see that, though the pressure of the jaws had drawn blood and must have hurt unbearably, no permanent damage had been done. Aside from a sizable patch of bloodstained fur and a thin, straight line where the skin had been torn, the paw appeared to be whole.

"Take a look at this," Mike said.

He reached up and opened the wolf's mouth, pulling at the

skin on its muzzle to expose rows of long, pure-white teeth. Mike poked at the wolf's jaw, examining different teeth and checking all the gum tissue to make sure the wolf hadn't hurt anything too badly while biting at the trap. He turned to me.

"Go ahead and touch them. Just don't stick your fingers too far inside."

I leaned down and held an open hand in front of the wolf's nose. His eyes weren't fully closed, and I wondered if somehow, from deep within his opiate cage, the wolf could see my palm, the sagebrush, and beyond it, the upended sky. The wolf took shallow, irregular breaths that passed hotly across my skin. I reached in and ran my index finger down the long edge of a canine. It was smooth, dry, and surprisingly warm to the touch. I worked my way backward, carefully tracing the outline of each tooth. After following the ascending pyramids of the sectoral teeth, noting how they increased in size as one went farther back, I skipped across to the great flat knife of the carnassial. Of a wolf's teeth, the carnassial is most fearsome by far. The canines are showy things, like paired stiletto knives, and they're essential for bringing down prey of any size. But once the chase is over, the carnassial teeth are where most of the work gets done. They're razor sharp, formed in the shape of a wide-based, double-peaked mountain. They look, in fact, quite like the rocky peak on the Paramount Pictures marquee. Carnassials are made for butchery. They slice through flesh and ligaments with ease. Along with their attendant molars, the carnassials can reduce an elk carcass to a pile of cracked, marrowless bones.

Mike muzzled the wolf, in case the drugs began wearing off before we finished collaring and collecting information. Handing me a clipboard with a data sheet, he began to call out things like the wolf's heart rate, temperature, age, and condition. I wrote hurriedly and helped Mike when I could, handing him vials for blood samples and assisting as he weighed the wolf with a sling and portable scale. Hanging suspended, the wolf seemed like a whole lot of predator for eighty-five pounds.

I prepped the collar, adjusting its size and sorting out the washers and nylon locknuts that held the device in place. When Mike wasn't looking, I scribbled down the radio frequency number from the back of the transmitter. I wrote it high on the inside of my arm, and then, supposing that sweat might render it illegible, I copied it into the little red book I carried to keep track of mineral sites and cattle ailments.

Mike probably would have given me the number if I had asked for it. We were, after all, the most conservation-minded ranch in the valley. Still, I worried that he might have balked because of some agency policy and I wasn't about to miss the chance to keep tabs on a new wolf. So I kept the number hidden.

Mike fit the collar, making it snug but not too tight, and I held it in place while he threaded a pair of small bolts through prepunched holes and screwed the locknuts down tight against thick leather. When we finished, Mike injected a reversing agent into the wolf's rump and we retreated a hundred yards to watch it take effect.

Ten minutes passed and I worried that the wolf would not wake. When he finally, blearily raised his head, I drew my first calm breath. He struggled to stand, tipped over once, and then stumbled like a drunk toward the mountains. As the wolf climbed uphill, he regained control of his legs. By the time he disappeared across the crest of the first foothill, he was trotting. Somewhere up there, his pack was waiting. They would welcome the yearling home, unaware that the strange, new device around his neck would broadcast their whereabouts.

———•·•———

Everything is information. Pat Zentz said that to me years ago while we were driving around his ranch looking for a mule deer that he could shoot. He said it first in the cab when the wind came up and started flattening the grass so that it pointed northeast, then again when we saw a fork-horn struggling out of a coulee in an advanced state of exhaustion. Worn-out and banged up, that deer had just been beaten in one of the fights related to the fall rut. He walked right by the pickup, not fifty yards away. I kept expecting Pat to shoot, but he just watched through the window and said again that everything was information. Later, after we had driven to the far side of the coulee, stalked into the wind, and killed a four-point buck among his harem, I had to admit that Pat was right.

Some people are dumb enough to pronounce this high country empty. They pull off the highway at the Madison Bend, belly up to the bar at the Griz, watch the baseball game for a while, and then ask without the barest hint of irony: How can you live out here? Nothing happens and there isn't anything to do.

Now I just shrug like I never thought about it before. They're not ready to understand that the land is a palimpsest, overwritten countless times with jumbled but decipherable script. Tracks in the dust, broken barbwire, the shifting wind, and the swirl of magpies and other scavenger birds as they rise from the dark tim-

ber—all these things carry meaning. With the right sort of attention, the land tells any story a person could want to hear.

But this knowing is dangerous, a kind of seduction. One time I
did explain the whole shebang to a tourist, ending with the asser-
tion that everything is information. When his eyes lit up as I explained how animals, storms, and seasons mark the land, I knew
that he was thinking of buying his own place in the Madison.
Like everybody else, he wanted a slice of paradise. Now I keep
my mouth shut, because twenty years of visiting the Zentz Ranch
taught me where talk like that can lead. The Billings exurbs have
crossed the Yellowstone River and crept up Duck Creek like a
flood tide. A spare, breathtaking landscape has become a vacuum
into which has rushed every sort of debris: plastic bags blow across
hayfields and snag on the right-of-way fences; headlights and gun-
shots carve up the night, leaving deer and cattle dead in the fields.
The detritus of city life—junk mail, broken toys, aluminum cans,
and soiled diapers—spill from the windows of passing cars and
collect in the roadside ditches.

This was the future I feared most deeply for the Sun Ranch.
Although the ranch had remained wild and largely untrammeled,
the same could not be said for the rest of the valley floor. A small
subdivision occupied half a section of land adjacent to the ranch's
northern boundary. It was just twenty or so houses spaced evenly
across three hundred and twenty acres, but it bothered me.

An image of those houses popped into my head when, hauling
salt to the heifers, I met a survey crew setting up their equipment
in the middle of an old hayfield. When I asked the foreman what
he was up there taking stock of, he responded enthusiastically.

"Oh, just about everything. We're working up a bunch of overlays for this place. Wildlife corridors, roads, utilities, viewsheds, streams and water rights, development potential—you name it, we're mapping it."

He asked me what I did for a living, and I told him.

"Agriculture," he replied. "We're doing a map for that, too. Maybe when we come back with a draft of this stuff you can give us some notes."

The surveyor seemed like a decent and capable man, but the word *development* sat poorly with me. I didn't stew about it for long, though. My fears about the future of the ranch were quickly eclipsed by the immediate tasks of tending herds, watching for wolves, and working all the daylight hours.

————•·•————

Around the middle of July we sorted off the bulls from Orville Skogen's replacement heifers. Skogen's bulls were almost identical—all ball sack, shit stains, and muscle—except for one. Among that homogenous crowd, one animal had worn the poll of his head bald from scrapping. The exposed skin was shockingly pale for a Black Angus, and from a distance the bare spot looked precisely like a tonsure. Once I noted the resemblance, it was hard to drive through the pastures without laughing at the sight of a black-robed monk enthusiastically screwing the heifers.

We sorted off the bulls and I trailed them along Badluck Way toward the pasture where they would graze for the rest of the summer. They started out rank. Fresh from breeding, they butted, scuffled, and raised dust from the gravel road. They took turns wheeling around to paw, bellow, and give me the eye. I was in charge of the bulls until shipping time and already it was going sour.

But then the bald bull moved out in front. He walked the roadside fence calmly and the other bulls followed. At the gate I stepped wide and he turned into the pasture without a backward glance. Because of his penchant for leading and the monastic hairdo, I decided to call him Moses.

Twice a week I took salt to the bulls and checked the water trough. I worked them a little bit from the four-wheeler, making each one take a few steps as I watched for signs of lameness. Each bull moved differently under pressure. Two usually trotted off, keeping a good distance away from me. Three others liked to turn to face the machine and make as if they would charge. The bald one always waited until I came within a few feet of him. When I was upwind he sniffed the air. I almost had to bump him to provoke a reluctant step back.

One day, mostly out of curiosity, I decided to shut off the engine, climb off the four-wheeler, and see how close I could get. The first step made me nervous, but then I noticed the softness in his eyes.

A ranch hand must be scarier afoot than on top of a clattering motor, at least to a bull. I could not walk within ten yards of him that first day or the next time I came with salt. But something kept me trying, and over the course of a few attempts, I shortened the distance between us. Soon we were separated by just a few feet.

I stood in the pasture with my arm outstretched, clutching a handful of fresh-pulled grass. The gesture would have looked absurd if anyone had been around to see it: we were in the midst of a green sea, an endless expanse of growth. Despite the fact that I offered only what he slept, walked, and shat on, Moses stretched his neck out and worked his nose double-time. He drew back whenever I reached forward, but as we repeated the motion, he retreated less and less. Soon the shoots were brushing across the wet tip of his nose, and then his tongue was snaking out, gathering the grass, and snatching it from my fingers.

I stopped awhile with Moses each time I went to check on the bulls and whenever I passed through his pasture on the way to somewhere else. I tore the grass from around my feet and held it out to him, and he took it.

Eventually I could scratch him on the neck and shoulders, and even lay my hand on the poll of his head—the spot he had scraped bald from fighting during breeding season—while he pressed gently back against it.

When my father came to visit I took him out to see Moses. In a photo he snapped I am bent over at the waist with my hands on the ground. My forehead is against that of a sleek black bull. It looks as though we are pushing against each other and I am winning. I showed the photo to Jeremy.

"That's a pretty stupid thing to do," he said. "That bull could sneeze and break your neck."

He went on to give me a list of good reasons why people don't give names to the livestock or play around with them, at least not on a spread this size. Most of them boiled down to this: singling something out with a name allows it to become unique. There is no room for this in the modern agricultural world, where efficiency has become the highest law and most calves never live to see their third birthday.

How It Started

*T*he sun edged above the Madison Range, warming the air. There was wind enough to rustle in the grass and keep the mosquitoes down. I was alone on horseback and had been riding toward what promised to be a perfect day when I found the heifer. She stood by herself in a meadow just below the fence that separated the ranch's deeded ground from the high pastures we leased from the Forest Service. Only a day had passed since we had gathered up all 790 of our heifers and pushed them southeast into the hills and convoluted valleys of Squaw Creek, so I wondered if she had jumped back or whether we might have left her behind when we moved the herd. I rode in close and began to walk her up a nearby fence.

But then I saw the bloody stripes just under and to the right of her tail. It took me a while to believe that they were there. Red is hard to see on black, and looking at her meant squinting toward the rising sun. It was only after I saw the rip in her bag, which closed and opened with each step, that I realized what had happened. I trailed her that way for a minute or so, thinking about my options. Some small part of me, knowing the chain of events that had been set in motion, was tempted to push the heifer into the forest and never say a word.

But the greater part burned with a rage that grew as I rode behind her. I watched the torn flesh above her udders yawn darkly open and drizzle blood in the dust. I noted the labored way she held her head and how she looked longingly over her shoulder at the lower pastures, where she had been safe.

It seemed that I had failed both wolf and cow by dint of my inability to prevent an attack. I pulled my radio from where it hung on my belt, put it to my lips, and said nothing. For a long moment I wondered what would be the right course of action. When nothing came of that, I settled for what was necessary: I pressed the talk button down.

"Jeremy," I said, "do you copy?"

His usual measured reply came quickly: "Go ahead."

We had to be cautious with the radio, since our repeater was capable of sending a signal nearly to Bozeman. Because I could never be sure who was listening, I chose my words with extreme care.

"We've got a situation up here. One heifer—torn up pretty bad. Over."

I waited, but nothing issued from the speaker. Finally, my radio came alive with static. It hissed for a few long seconds, enough time for me to picture Jeremy standing outside the Moose Creek shop with the talk button pressed down, putting his answer together.

When Jeremy finally replied, he sounded tight and monotone, as though speaking through clenched teeth.

"What's your twenty?" he asked.

"On the road, below the Squaw Creek fence."

"Stay right with her," he said. "I'll be up in a minute with the trailer. Over."

A minute, it turned out, wasn't too far off. I turned back toward the heifer and tried to read the number on her ear tag. When I looked back down the road, I could see a dust plume rising high into the blue sky.

Jeremy skidded to a stop beside me and stepped down to take stock of things. The heifer watched nervously as he walked in a slow circle. When Jeremy got straight behind her, he stopped and let out a low whistle.

"The sons of bitches," he said. "She's done."

We parked the trailer in the middle of a nearby gate and, after a few clumsy, bloody attempts, got her to step inside. Jeremy told me to make a short loop through the pasture to look for other casualties, then head down to meet him at the Wolf Creek shop.

I rode slowly toward the Squaw Creek hogback. At a corner in the fence, I found a wire gate torn to shreds and thoroughly trampled. The damage looked too extensive to be the work of a single heifer—even one with a pack of wolves behind her—and so I rode through the gate to see what I could find.

The heifers hadn't gone far. No more than a half mile from the gate they stood high on a hillside, bunched together in a tight group. Figuring they'd be wild and ready to bolt, I rode a wide circle before starting to ease them back uphill. None looked to be gravely injured. They had, however, been harassed in the night and it showed. Up close the heifers looked exhausted. They moved in jerky fits and starts, sticking together and balking when I pressed them uphill toward the broken gate and the mountains.

I rode back down, unsaddled my horse in the barn, and met up with James and Jeremy. Listening to them talk, I realized that the course of our summer had been irrevocably changed by the morning's discovery.

Jeremy had already reported the attack to Montana Fish, Wildlife & Parks. FWP, in turn, had contacted Wildlife Services, a division of the U.S. Department of Agriculture tasked with predator control. For their part, Wildlife Services pledged to send a government trapper to the ranch, to verify the attack and discuss potential courses of action. In the meantime, we were instructed to keep the heifer alive if possible.

James and Jeremy rode all afternoon, checking on the cattle. I watched as each of them lashed a rifle scabbard to his saddle. Jeremy took the Tikka .243 he always kept in his work truck. James brought an old .30-.30 that he once told me was his first real gun. I strapped our radio receiver to the front rack of the four-wheeler, loaded up the back with wire and fencing tools, and then headed uphill to fix the ruined gate.

Up there I switched the receiver on and made a thorough sweep of the hills. I tried every frequency: Rotten Teeth, the newly collared yearling, and two more that belonged to a pack from the Gravelly side. When my efforts yielded nothing but the hiss and crackle of static, I started in on the gate.

Since most of the wooden stays were broken and all the wires were snapped, I decided to rebuild the thing from scratch. I worked with the volume on my ranch radio turned all the way up, so I could hear James and Jeremy talking as they checked the herd.

A wire gate is simple. In all it consists of five barbwires strung between two stout end stays, with a few lesser sticks in between to maintain the spacing of the strands. The gate hangs between two H-braces, secured to each of them by loops of wire. One end is rigged to open, with loops that can slip off the top and bottom of the end stay.

Stringing up a bunch of wires is easy. Building a good gate— one tight enough to stop stock, loose enough to be opened by most people, and sturdy enough to stay that way for years—is an art.

I began by fastening loops of smooth wire around the posts of the H-braces. I made four, one for the top and bottom of each side. As I twisted wire and drove staples, I tracked James's and Jeremy's progress through a landscape I knew by heart. I listened when Jeremy laid claim to riding the high loop—up over the hogback and along the big ridge that separated the forks of Squaw Creek. He sent James on a lower trail—down through the timber along the North Fork of the creek.

The radios went silent for a while, and I immersed myself in the work of fencing. Choosing two straight poles for stays, I trimmed them to the right size with a chain saw and stuck them through the wire loops at either end of the gate's opening. I pulled a heavy spool of barbwire from the four-wheeler, secured one end to a stay, and rolled more of it out across the ground. I snipped it off with my fencing pliers and used a wire stretcher—an ingenious metal ratchet that can put hundreds of pounds of pressure on a strand—to snug up the wire. With the stretcher's help, I looped the tail of my wire twice around the end stay and then tied it off with four tight twists.

I strung the top wire, then the bottom one. After tightening each strand, I checked the tension of the gate by pressing my shoulder against the end stay and slipping off the wire loop. From time to time I heard James and Jeremy raise each other on the radio.

"James, what's your twenty? Over."

"I'm still working down the North Fork. Not seeing much for cattle. Over."

"Plenty up here, but they're all bunched up. Over and out."

They fell silent for a while and I strung my last three wires. I added a few stays to the inner span of the gate, marking the wire spacing out on each. Just as I began to staple up the wires, James's voice boomed out of my radio.

"Jeremy, you copy?"

"Go ahead."

"You better get down here. It's . . ."

The radio kept up a thin, crackling whisper.

"It's a wreck."

He was down at the water gap, a spot where the fence jogged back and forth across the creek so that animals on either side of it could drink from the same stream. Before James signed off, he asked if I could hear him.

"Go ahead," I said.

"You're gonna want to come down here, too. Bring the receiver."

I drove along a bench that ran roughly parallel to the North Fork of Squaw Creek, figuring that when the going got tough I could walk the rest of the way down to the water gap. I parked the four-wheeler where the land dropped off, unstrapped the receiver, and started to hurry downhill. Fifty yards above the creek, I skidded to a stop on top of a little ridge with a big view.

From up there I could see it all. James, off his horse, stood beside Squaw Creek. Upstream of him, a black heifer lay sprawled, bloated, and partially consumed—half in and half out of the water. Not far above her on the hillside, jammed into a ninety-degree corner in the fence, a group of ten or so heifers stood paralyzed with fear.

———

We wrapped the heifer's carcass in a plastic tarp and weighted the edges down with stones. The idea was to make it look unfamiliar enough to deter scavengers, and preserve the body until the government hunter could come and declare a cause of death. It worked that day and the carcass was undisturbed when we brought Chad out to see it in the morning.

Confident and square-jawed, Chad was a man who had found

the right line of work. He wore no recognizable uniform, just a snap shirt, faded Wranglers, and a pair of boots with slight military overtones. Chad loved to track, trap, hunt, and kill predators—wolves most of all. He had, in fact, been a hunting guide before he went to work for the USDA. To hear him tell it, after their reintroduction to Yellowstone, the wolves had gobbled up most of the trophy elk in the drainages where he used to take clients, eating him out of a job.

Jeremy led Chad down to the body, and I joined them there after making a short lap through the herd. Chad pulled out a small pocketknife and began to skin the heifer, looking for bite marks and bruising beneath the hide. Since the hair and thick skin of cattle tend to hide damage, peeling the body was often the best way to determine how an animal had died. The presence or absence of hemorrhaging also indicated whether the heifer had been alive or dead when the wounds were inflicted.

He started skinning at the base of the skull and worked his way down from there. I marveled at the effortless way he stripped hide from flesh and how little mess it made. Chad went looking for damage and found it in spades. Beneath the heifer's black shroud of hide, she was stippled with a hundred canine-tooth punctures. Some of the holes in her neck and high on her flanks were ringed with bright blood, confirming that she still had a heartbeat when they were made.

"Definitely wolves," Chad muttered. "Not that you guys were wondering."

Chad walked over to a five-gallon bucket and began pulling out leghold traps. Thinking he was going to be at it for a few minutes, I sat down on the trunk of a fallen tree. He must have seen the movement, because Chad wheeled around.

"Don't sit!" he snapped.

I jumped up as though bitten.

"Every spot we touch—they smell it. Set your ass on something and they'll know from a mile away."

He went back to fiddling with the traps. After a while, he turned to Jeremy and said pointedly:

"I'm going to be at this for a while."

Taking the hint, we left him to his work. As we walked out, Jeremy filled me in on a couple of things. First, he said that we had been authorized by the state to shoot two wolves on sight. Second, he told me that when Chad volunteered to fill our permits from a government helicopter, Roger had told him no.

Killing would be done, Jeremy said, and unless Chad's traps caught something in the next couple of days, the ranch crew would do it. The hope was that, by chasing the wolves on the ground or trapping them off a carcass, our retribution against the pack would be less capricious. We might be able to kill strategically and drive the pack far back into the mountains in the process.

From then on, time picked up speed until events and actions ran together like watercolor. There seemed never to be enough time between sunrise and sunset. I did chores with my eyes on the foothills and slept in the back of my truck beside the cattle.

Not long after the first attack, James and his family started staying nights in a little cabin up Squaw Creek. The shack was without electricity and running water, and getting to it meant a long, jostling trip along grown-in two-track roads. If he or his family ever missed the comforts of home, I never heard them complain. Over a campfire dinner up there, James told me that he would do all he could to keep the heifers safe, and the wolves on the run.

He was as good as his word, and wore out horses in the course of keeping tabs on the herd.

When I think of these things, or anything else from the end of July, it is impossible to escape two images from a dream I had at the time. The first is a pile of dead heifers that grows each time I look at it. All are in states of decay and consumption. Some are bloated and some are bones. The second image is a low, gray wolf-shadow, moving constantly through the corner of the frame.

A little before dusk, the wolf crossed through Squaw Creek's dense timber, stepping lightly over toppled logs and detouring to avoid the soft, treacherous ground near seeps and water holes. He moved cautiously, eschewing well-worn trails for more tangled routes. From time to time he stopped to watch his pack mates find their own ways through the brush.

Change had come swiftly: one morning, the wolves returned from a fruitless night hunt and bedded down at the confluence of the North and Middle Fork. Within hours, cattle began arriving by the hundreds. Bunched up in tight, bawling scrums, heifers walked out of the low country and into the foothills. Riders and dogs followed the herds, pressing them toward the scattered timber and lush grass of the mountains.

Cattle spread across the landscape like a hardy, alien weed, trampling grass and leaving massive shit piles at the creek crossings where they came to water. At first, unnerved by all the dust, bustle, and noise, the pack steered clear, retreating toward the South Fork of Squaw Creek, the most remote and impenetrable corner of their domain.

The sun was gone and the twilight fading by the time the wolf crossed the long, stony ridge that stands like a battlement between the South Fork and the rest of the valley. He chose to follow a familiar trail, sniffing at important trees and pissing often to mark his passage. Behind him, the other wolves staked their claims in similar fashion. Down where the trail crossed an old logging road, he picked up a fresh scent and decided to follow it.

It was full dark by the time the wolf found a small bunch of heifers grazing in a meadow above the North Fork. A dozen bovine heads jerked to attention when he stepped from the timber. For a moment, nothing moved. The cattle did not spring away and vanish like deer, or gather up and run together like elk. The wolf took a single step forward. One heifer pawed the ground and shook her head from side to side. Another let out a low, guttural noise like a cough, spun on her hind hooves, and disappeared into the forest.

Her panic was contagious, and it scattered the rest of the herd. Heifers ran pell-mell in all directions, snapping branches in their hurried flight. In an instant the wolf was running, closing the gap between himself and the nearest yearling. The pack was at his heels, and they pulled her swiftly to earth.

The wolves ate well that night, and they learned something. From then on they looked differently at the strange creatures that had come into their mountains.

The Brush Gun

*T*he Bad Luck spring box needed to be checked every day, wolves or no. I sat beside it staring up at the foothills and the gray stone peaks behind them. With the volume high on my radio, I could listen to the others talking as they hunted. James and Jeremy discussed the location of fresh sign. James had heard howling early in the morning.

My world had filled up to the brim with wolves. I watched for them all day while I worked, and when I had to piss I did it on the gateposts and trees they used to mark territory. In the evening I went home, ate a quick dinner, and drove out again to sleep among cows and listen for the far-off howling of the pack.

We checked cattle obsessively. Day after day I went out on horseback to ride through the steers and heifers. I borrowed one of Jeremy's rifles, slung it across my back, and spent hours with the herds. At home when I took off my shirt and looked in the mirror, my lower back was bruised purple in the shape of breech and bolt.

James and Jeremy made their own rounds. Both were practiced hunters, having each brought down their share of deer, elk, and other game. They had camouflage coats, good binoculars, familiar guns, and scabbards to carry them in. They did not have to practice the movements of chambering a round or check endlessly to see whether the safety was off or on, as I did.

Someone once told me that wolves travel in circles. In a book on the species, a map showed the movement of three packs as lines with directional arrows and dated waypoints. The packs overlapped their routes like the Venn diagrams that demonstrate a gray area.

Each pack ran an enormous circuit over the course of a week or ten days. While they don't end up in the same place each Wednesday or use a specific trail, wolves tend to visit and revisit the outer extremes of their territories. They follow the same general course through their landscape, diverging from it according to circumstance and season.

We couldn't say how our pack was moving, but we kept missing them and they kept killing. Every day or two for a week we gathered around another dead heifer, looked for sign, and went off with our guns in hand. We dispersed to search along the edges and inside the wildest nooks of the ranch. We patrolled our territory.

Of the three of us, I was the least interested in shooting a wolf. For Jeremy, each new dead cow meant listening to another one of Orville Skogen's tantrums. Every loss had to be reported over the phone and, though I never got to listen in, I doubted that the conversion of a cool thousand dollars into wolf shit did much to improve Orville's thorny disposition. More and more it seemed like Jeremy's reputation as a ranch foreman was on the line and each wolfless day tarnished it.

James was a born hunter—better at stalking and killing things by the end of his teens than most people get to be in a lifetime. Hunting wolves was a rare opportunity for him, something not to be missed, but that wasn't the whole of it. James was a cattleman through and through. He loved his herds unstintingly, and wholeheartedly devoted himself to their protection and care. James liked wildlife, too—enjoyed seeing, living among, and hunting it—but his first loyalty was always to the stock.

I was less sure about the whole undertaking, stuck between a love of wild things and rage at the ruin of a summer's work. I kept out of the hunt for a while, attending instead to the ranch's day-to-day tasks. I carried a gun, sure, but doubted whether I could pull the trigger if a wolf walked through the sights. While James and Jeremy hunted, I hauled salt to the cattle, spliced wires, and cleaned stock tanks.

One night, as July ground through its final week, something inside me gave way. I bedded down beside the cattle, arranged my gun and other things, and then stared straight up into a vaulted dome of stars for hours. Though I was exhausted, I could not sleep. Perhaps it was the result of the endless workdays, the terror I glimpsed in the eyes of certain cows, or the vivid carnage that the wolves left in their wake. I stayed awake with muscles tense and fists clenched tight, watching the progress of a thin crescent moon. When morning finally came, I was seething with anger. The wolves had gone too far. They had stolen too much from us.

On the twenty-eighth, with a total of four heifers dead and the wolves still maddeningly elusive, Jeremy decided to make a big push through the timbered folds of Squaw Creek. I volunteered to come along. He just nodded and then, when James was out of earshot for a moment, asked:

"If you see a wolf, do I have your word that you'll shoot it?"

I thought a moment, and then told him that I would. James returned and handed me a rifle, the old Winchester .30-.30 he'd bought at the age of twelve.

"It's a brush gun," he said. "Perfect for that thick timber in Squaw Creek."

I looked over the gun carefully. It was a well-used lever action, bereft of ornamentation and engraving. The wooden stock was dinged in a few places, but freshly sealed with oil. I practiced throwing it to my shoulder and looking down the barrel, wondering when it had last been fired or sighted in. I loaded five shells into the tubular magazine. We rode out on four-wheelers before I could take a practice shot.

We walked for hours in the roughest sort of country. I climbed through a hundred deadfall thickets and splashed across the North and Middle Forks of Squaw Creek. All the while I could not shake the feeling that the wolves were just ahead, hidden by thick timber and tricks of light and shadow. Though I carried no food and always seemed to pick difficult, steep, and circuitous routes, I did not tire. A strange force pulled me onward. It kept my eyes peeled and my feet moving fast. I drank from clean little springs, feeling always as though I was not alone.

I wish it had been otherwise. I wish I could say that I hunted the wolves reluctantly. That pursuing them through the maze of Squaw Creek was a hard but necessary duty. That might sound right, but it would be a lie. The truth is that, once I lost sight of James and Jeremy, chasing wolves afoot gave me a feeling I've never had before or since. It sharpened my sight and brushed cobwebs from every corner of my mind. It focused me so intensely on the task of pursuit that everything else faded away. I did not notice the passing of the afternoon, or that I teetered on the threshold of exhaustion, until I met up with James and Jeremy on a ridge above the thick swath of forest where the South Fork of Squaw Creek seeped into the world.

We stood there, ragged and empty-handed, and looked down at the timber. The copse wasn't huge, measuring perhaps a half mile on its nearer side.

"Let's hunt through there," Jeremy said, "then call it a day."

We split up again. James would circle around the top end of the trees. Jeremy would walk a lower route, then lie in ambush on the far side. My instructions were to wait fifteen minutes and then walk smack through the middle, hopefully flushing the pack into the open. On the far side of the trees we'd meet up on an old two-track, then walk back home together.

I waited and then slid down a steep embankment into a night-mare of mud, old bones, and dripping water. The first step sank me past the knee. After that I walked on rotting trunks, exposed roots, and thick hummocks of moss. The bog was claustrophobic enough to set my hair on end. I ran the .30-.30's lever action, set the hammer at half cock, and tried to keep from falling. After a little while I found the slumping traces of an overgrown logging road and followed it into the heart of the bog. I remember green profusion, fallen trees, and shadow. Through this, deft and mas-sive, came the wolf.

We saw each other simultaneously and then, though I can't re-call lifting the gun or thumbing back the hammer, I fired. The bul-let knocked him over, and when he struggled up, I could see that his hind end was ruined. With his front paws, the wolf dragged toward the shelter of thick underbrush. I shot again and hit a tree. Again, and he tumbled out of view. I rushed downhill past blood-stains on a pine and came upon him breathing out his last in a clearing not ten feet across. He seemed to fill it.

I racked in another cartridge and hesitated, wondering whether to give him a few more moments or shoot again to kill quickly. But by the time my thought had passed, he was gone and I was alone in the clearing with nothing but the shot ringing in my ears. The others started calling on the radio and crashing toward me through the muck and downed timber. Sick to my stomach, I sat at the clearing's edge and stared at the body.

———•◦•———

The carcass had to be inspected by scientists from Fish, Wildlife & Parks. Doubting their ability to navigate through the depths of the South Fork, we decided to carry the wolf out to a little two-track road. Jeremy tied the paws together with baling twine—hind and front. James found a stout branch, broke the limbs off, and threaded it between the wolf's legs. They leaned against trees and tried to cheer me up.

"He's a big one, a hundred pounds—maybe the alpha male," said James. "People would pay money to hunt a wolf like that."

"Probably got a belly full of steak," Jeremy added.

He clapped me on the back. "You did good."

I nodded dumbly, said nothing. James and Jeremy discussed the next move and wondered aloud if this would be enough to drive the pack into the mountains. They smiled and talked as if we were not sharing the clearing with a dead body and the echoes of atrocity.

They handed me their rifles, went to the wolf, and lifted the pole onto their shoulders. I walked ahead of them, searching in vain for an easy path out of the bog.

After a few minutes I switched places with Jeremy and brought up the rear of our procession. The pole was not much longer than the wolf, which meant I had to walk close to its voided asshole in a cloud of dog-shit stench. Once, when James stopped abruptly, I almost stepped face-first into it.

It felt like a shortcut through hell. James and I moved clumsily, tripping over branches and sinking in the mud. The wolf became an awful pendulum, lurching back and forth between us. As we stumbled along, I couldn't stop thinking about the fact that I had taken something that floated through the forest like a spirit, and reduced it to dead weight and a fecal smell. At last we reached the little dirt road that followed Squaw Creek down toward the highway and left the body there, beside a boulder. We would call Fish, Wildlife & Parks, so they could send someone up in the morning to collect the carcass for necropsy.

James insisted on taking a picture of me with the wolf. I knelt behind it and he snapped two shots with a disposable camera.

"You okay?" he asked.

I nodded, and when he looked away, I reached down, used my knife to slice a few long hairs from the wolf's tail, and tucked them in my pocket.

The Silence That Followed

Sleep was out of the question. After dinner I paced back and forth in the bunkhouse, growing more agitated every time I passed the front door. Without really knowing why, I laced up my boots, grabbed my shotgun and a flashlight, and headed out into the night.

I drove fast down the highway and turned through the gate at Squaw Creek, the truck a speck of light moving across the new-moon blackness of the foot-hills, winding upward toward the Madison Range. Ahead the stretched oval of the headlights illuminated two dirt ruts and the rough bark of pines on either side. Beyond that the darkness was opaque, impenetrable.

I got out to open a gate and a chill passed over me that felt out of place on a late-July night. I pulled the truck through and went to close the gate behind it. From the rear, the taillights seemed like the last things left over from another world. I couldn't shake the feeling that they were about to wink out.

I drove to where we had left the wolf earlier in the day, stretched out at the base of a pale boulder, just off the left-hand side of the road. He was straight-legged and silver in the headlight glare, and I watched closely from the cab as though he might move. A thin line of blood snaked between the wolf's back teeth, crossed his dark-gray muzzle, and clumped in the dust. It curved like a creek leaving the mountains.

I could not stop seeing the kill. The wolf emerged again and again from the trees. Each time, I shouldered the rifle and squeezed the trigger, living again the explosion, the impact, and the ringing silence that followed.

I glanced up from the body to the stone and then into the darkness behind it. I used to like walking these foothills and ex-ploring the wild country where Squaw Creek leaks out of the Madisons. Up here, only two months before, I had seen my first wolf, a far shadow trotting the edge of the forest, dipping in and out of the sunlight, moving so fast and beautifully that I for-got myself. I was supposed to have yelled, waved my arms, and charged it, but I let the wolf pass. It was silent and silver-gray, like the body.

I slid from the truck and took a step forward. Against the boulder, in the high beams, the wolf glowed cold as the moon. His half-closed eyes were green. Besides the blood they were the only color.

When my hand broke the plane of the headlights, it turned yellow. I held it up and watched it burn against the wolf. Projected on the boulder's face, my five-fingered shadow started out huge and diminished as I walked forward. Just before I knelt over the wolf and sank my fingers in his mane, I noticed that my hands were shaking.

I burrowed downward through the long, kinked guard hairs and the finer white ones underneath until my fingertips touched cold skin. I reached toward his shoulder and did it again. Again. What stopped me was a little whorl in his coarse rib fur. I knew it at a touch—beneath was a hole, ragged flesh, and shattered bone. It was too much. I stood up, stepped out of the headlights, and waited for the night breeze to lick my fingers dry.

———•◦•———

"How do you get over a thing like that?" An old friend of mine asked the question over the phone, and I couldn't answer him. I know what I did after killing the wolf, which was take two days off, drive down to Jackson Hole, speak to nobody, drink hard, and try to forget about it.

When I got back to the bunkhouse, it seemed that the ranch had managed to return to something like normality. In my absence James had killed a wolf of his own, thereby filling our second "shoot on sight" permit. He'd made a clean job of it, Jeremy told me, using just a single bullet. The wolf never knew what hit it.

If Jeremy was less than pleased that James had used the permit on a subadult, he never said so to me. In fact, attacking the young of the year might have been what finally pushed the Wedge Pack over the edge. After the second killing, they made a beeline for the mountains. Jeremy went out with the radio receiver one evening and heard a few faint clicks from the direction of Finger Lake and Expedition Pass. After that, there was nothing.

How do you get over something like the wolf? You don't, really. Working like a madman helps, so I immersed myself in ranching. I herded and settled cattle that the wolves had scattered. I watched diligently for signs of infection and disease. When I found anything suspicious, I helped James and Jeremy rope and doctor animals back to health. I slept out nights and listened for howling that never came. Having nearly exhausted the ranch's supply of broken fences, I spent large chunks of time in the saddle and worked on my horsemanship and herding skills in earnest.

Jeremy took notice. He split up the cattle between James and me. From that point on, taking care of the steers was my primary responsibility. James, in turn, looked after the heifers. Around the same time, Jeremy let me start riding his horse, Billy.

What a thing it was to ride that big, quick-legged gelding out through dew-soaked grass in the early morning. Billy covered as much ground at a walk as most horses do trotting. He brought the horizon underfoot in a flash and never seemed to tire.

I rode. I herded. I set out salt and mineral, immersing myself in the lives and health of cattle until little time remained to think of anything else. Slowly, over weeks, the wolf began to fade. By mid-September, I could shut my eyes and go to sleep without seeing blood, fur, and bullets.

– IV –

THE LONG
MONTHS

What Remains

*J*eremy once told me about a young man who rode for a grazing association in mountains southeast of the Sun. By all accounts the man was kind, quiet, and exceptionally skilled with a lasso. At the end of a long day he sat with the other hands by the fire, listening as they talked about cattle and women and watching sparks climb.

"I wish I were a better horseman," he said, then stood and went out from the firelight into the mountain dark. When a single pistol shot rang out, the others knew the noise for what it was.

The dead man left relics: work clothes, a saddle, and horses. Once, on the way into town, Jeremy pointed out a truck that had belonged to the departed cowboy. I stared at that orphaned Chevy until we rounded the next bend.

Not long afterward, my mother visited the ranch and tagged along to watch me work. I walked a fence line, splicing wire and pounding staples while she waited. When I returned, she held out her hand to show me an elk vertebra as white as ivory. She said:

"There are so many bones here. You just don't see them until you sit still."

From a distance, the grassy benches and foothills of this valley look austere and empty. Up close there are as many bones as bunchgrasses. It is a strange trick of decomposition: Soft tissue turns black and melts into the earth, leaving no record except a striking, oval-shaped green-up in the spring. Bones remain. They stay in place after the initial violence of stripping and disarticulation, accumulating over years.

Fallen-down homesteads, gray, slump-roofed, and chinked with scraps of newspaper from World War I, are bones. So are dry ditches going nowhere and slowly filling in, liquor bottles by the highway, boarded windows on the outskirts of town, and houses that can be sold only to strangers. We live with bones and keep making more.

———————

In late summer, James and I were riding south through the foothills. More relaxed than we had been in a month, we traveled toward Squaw Creek with his dog Bee trotting behind. The Wedge Pack, so far as we could tell, had left the ranch and retreated into the farthest recesses of the Lee Metcalf Wilderness. Westward, we could see our herd grazing in high grass. Beyond them were miles and miles of open air and then the dark-green humpback of the Gravelly Range. To the east the Madisons stuck up so close and stark and rugged they could have been the painted set from a cowboy movie. We tried for a shortcut through the creek bottom, where the pines were dense enough to get lost in. Our horses labored through, plunging over deadfall and snapping minor branches.

In the really thick stuff, we found where the wolves had killed a six-point bull elk. His skull lay fifty feet from his rib cage. Both were stark white against the moss. Looking at the bones, James said it must have happened during winter. I shuddered to imagine this place choked up with snow, with the bull spinning clumsy posthole turns to keep the pack at bay.

We climbed out of the creek bottom, our horses blowing, and as we gained the top of a long, open ridge, James saw a skunk in the grass ahead. He drew the little Walther .22 that he carried everywhere and handed it to me. It was a silly-looking gun—a green plastic semiautomatic, small enough to fit in the palm of my hand. "Shoot that thing before it sprays the dog," he said.

The skunk waddled away from us, tail in the air. It was leaving, but not in a hurry. The last animals I had shot were the wolf and a maimed heifer. The heifer dropped like a stone and breathed out one long sigh that seemed almost relieved. The wolf had not quit darkening my dreams.

I handed the gun back to James and told him that if stinking had become a capital offense, he better save a bullet for each of us. He shrugged and muttered something, then goosed his horse forward and shot *pop-pop-pop-pop* until the skunk crumpled in a heap.

As the echoes faded, I saw movement out of the corner of my eye and turned to watch Bee disappear into the trees, headed back the way we came. She ran flat-out with her nub of a tail tucked. "Darn," James said as he spurred his horse ahead. He had three dogs and all of them were gun-shy.

———•••———

On his last workday, James and I took the four-wheelers up to the North End together. Our rigs were loaded down with sacks of salt, and we drove a big clockwise circle around the Flats. It was Friday, and on Sunday, James and his family were headed back to their house on the Utah-Idaho border for his final year of college.

I was staying. A week before, Roger had offered me a permanent job and I had taken it, agreeing to work through the winter and into next spring. I got a raise, from $1,650 to $1,800 a month, and health insurance. Jeremy said I could move out of the bunkhouse and into the little log house we called the Wolf Shack. Not bad for a ranch hand.

As we whizzed across the ranch, past cattle grazing in dark bunches and mountains scraping up against a clear blue sky, James must have been a little jealous. He was headed for the world of examinations and fluorescent light, while I got to stick around and have adventures.

We were gripped by separate euphorias. James was making the most of his last moment in the sun. He spun doughnuts through the grass and club moss and caught air across more than one ditch. I followed him, ecstatic in the knowledge that I did not have to leave and could work the ranch for years if I wanted. I pictured myself toiling until my body wore out, then buying a cabin by the river.

We drove fast, scattering cattle. I raced south toward the bench above Wolf Creek, and then watched James bail off the edge.

I followed him. That, after all, had been my policy all summer, and it had worked well. The slope looked steeper than anything I had yet descended, but I reasoned that if James could do it, I could, too. I shifted my weight back, dropped the transmission into first gear, and headed straight down.

A lot can happen in the weightless moments between a mistake and its consequences. I looked down as the front left tire hit a basketball-sized rock. I felt the back wheels leave the ground.

The four-wheeler rolled forward into space, and the ground rushed toward me. There was time enough to glance downhill and see James watching with a look of horror, time to realize that people die this way and to think bitterly that the rear rack was empty, the front one was full, and all this was happening because I forgot to balance a load of cow salt.

I hit hard, facedown, with the four-wheeler rolling over me. The handlebars bent against my shoulders, and a crushing weight pressed into the small of my back. I could not draw a breath. The four-wheeler moved on, flipping end over end downhill. I lay with my head against a rock as James climbed toward me.

In the city you call an ambulance for something like that. You keep the victim still until the paramedics arrive with a backboard. On Wolf Creek, James waited until I could take a normal breath, and then we talked it over. I could feel and move my legs, so he flipped my four-wheeler right side up and I rode it back to the shop.

Later, in Ennis, the doctor checked me for internal bleeding.

"Bruised ribs," he said. "You're lucky."

He told me a handful of stories about other people who hadn't been.

———·•·———

James owned the cattle dog on paper, but it was his wife, Kendra, who had raised him from a pup. She had nursed Tick back to health after a horse stepped on him and broke all his ribs, so it was she who had to give the dog away. Kendra had loved Tick from the beginning, but when she and James decided to start breeding border collies, the heeler had to go. They offered him to me.

They couldn't have failed to notice that I liked Tick. Often, after work, I would spring the dog from his kennel and take him jogging in the hills. They must also have guessed that winter on the Sun Ranch would be lonely, and figured that a dog would be better than nothing. After a couple of days' deliberation, I accepted.

Tick was strange, even among the muttish race of cattle dogs. His coat wasn't the usual merle or grizzled red, but deep brown with a light-gray frost—like a chocolate truffle rolled through ashes. He was taller, leggier, than most heelers, with a half mask and disproportionately large head. That head was always the first thing to catch a person's attention—a blocky, equilateral triangle, made mostly of jaw and teeth. From certain angles, it looked almost crocodilian.

James and Kendra made me a present of the dog and then left the ranch in a rattling convoy, bouncing down the gravel road to Highway 287. In spite of the pain from my ribs, I waved at the vehicles until they disappeared and then watched the road dust settle. Tick stood by my side and wagged his bobbed nub of a tail in the new and perfect silence.

A week or so later, James called me on the phone. He wanted to know if I was healing and how Tick was working out. I told him things were going well on both fronts. Tick had a new collar, a dog bed, and several other egregious luxuries. After a few initial moments of linoleum-induced panic, he had decided that he could get used to the indoor life. My ribs had improved to the point where I could make my rounds through the cattle, ride a horse, and breathe deep without much pain.

"That's great," said James, and then launched into a story about riding in his hometown rodeo. He was back behind the chutes, sorting out his rope and gear, getting ready for an event. A man rode up to him on horseback, with a pristine black Stetson and a brand-new pearl-snap shirt. James recognized the guy, though he couldn't think of his name, as a salesman from the car dealership downtown. The man rode up, shot James a look of contempt, and said something to the effect of "Get out of here—you ain't no cowboy."

James's laugh boomed through the phone. "Guess it was because he hadn't seen me there before."

James described the classes he was taking at Utah State and which bits of them applied to the Sun Ranch. In the midst of a case study in which cattle had been conditioned to seek out and consume invasive weeds, he stopped abruptly to ask:

"Have you seen the wolves around?"

I hadn't seen or heard them. Our radio receiver, despite regular use, hadn't picked up a signal from any of the Wedge Pack collars.

"Well, that's good. How's things otherwise?"

Listening to static on the line, I thought about how best to answer. For several evenings I had been walking up Moose Creek to listen in vain for the pack and mourn the wolf that I had taken from the world. Each night, as the sun's glow faded and no howling broke the silence, I headed home with grief and guilt sitting heavy as stones in my chest. Though I wanted to tell James all this, I supposed he'd understand none of it.

"Except for the dog," I finally said, "it's quiet."

A Hard Wind

*F*all swept into the Madison Valley in a hurry, as though anxious to be farther south. One morning I woke to find hoarfrost on my truck's windshield. By the next afternoon the aspens were turning yellow-gold from the low country up, gorgeously dotting and banding the landscape. For a week, maybe more, it lasted. The air was clear, crisp as the first bite of an apple. I relished it and rode when I could, trotting my horse along the old irrigation ditch to the North End Flats, where our heifer herd was finishing out the grazing season.

Tick trotted alongside, and when it came time to move cattle, he ran enthusiastic arcs behind them, harrying the stragglers and magnifying my impact on the stock. The dog stayed in constant motion, seeming never to tire. With Tick's help, I gathered hundreds of heifers into tight bunches and moved them across the breadth of the Flats in search of good grass. Those were the best days.

Mostly, though, because James was gone and I had miles to cover, I had to take the four-wheeler and vibrate across the landscape in a haze of dust and noise. One morning in late September I gassed it up, loaded the front and rear racks with sacks of salt, and buzzed out to the Flats under an overcast sky. Going north, I had the wind in my face, colder than it had been since spring, with a new bite that licked through the weave of my Carhartt and raised goose bumps. It came in wild, urgent gusts, panting like a messenger with bad news.

Nuzzled down into my collar, I turned north from Badluck Way, buzzed past a spot where the bulls stood bunched together, and dropped down to the North End Flats to find our heifer herd dotting the range like flies on a picnic table. At intervals there were other, lower specks in the grass, truck tires surrounded by ten-foot circles of bare dirt and cow shit. I stopped at the first one and shut off the engine, then sliced into two fifty-pound sacks— one straight salt and the other a rust-colored blend of minerals. I poured them side by side into the old tire, listening to the gentle rain sound the grains made against the salt tub's plywood bottom. I stirred the two colors together with my boot, muting each with the other. When I looked up, the heifers were ringed around me.

I moved across the Flats, salting the tires and then watching the heifers converge to orient themselves like filings around the pole of a magnet. I bent down to fill the last tub, and stood up in a blizzard.

Snow was nothing new. On the ranch it snowed every month of the year except August. There might have been a flurry that August, but I don't remember it. At six thousand feet, a dusting, even at the height of summer, is unremarkable. But this was altogether different from a summer snowstorm. The wind pushed harder, flattening the bluebunch and forcing my eyes shut. Snow fell sideways, pricking my skin and melting in spots usually protected by my hat brim. Flakes sped toward the ground at acute angles, so close together that it seemed there was more substance than space in between.

Northward there was no horizon, just a blurred-out space where the grass and the sky dissolved into white unity. I cupped a gloved hand across my eyes and peered out through the fingers. I walked forward into the wind for a few steps, and then glanced down to find my chest, jacket, and pants coated with pure, unbroken white.

I turned south and found the tub, the heifers, and the front end of the four-wheeler covered. Against the storm they seemed tentative, like studies or recollections of the things they were. The heifers held their heads above the salt tub, staring at me as if awaiting instructions. None moved or lowed or, so far as I could see, breathed. We had been swallowed by the storm—whitewashed and frozen together.

For a moment I was sure, dead sure, that I wouldn't escape. The white would draw tighter around us. It would fill the air until we choked on it, and then blanch our insides. The four-wheeler was nothing but an artifact, a line drawing. It would not start.

Then a heifer moved. Before the snowfall she would have been a Black Angus, slick-coated, wide-eyed, and fat. Now she dropped a ghost's muzzle into the tire and kept it there. I waited nervously. Her movement was a hope.

Her head rose slowly. Ears, eyes, and the long bridge of nose emerged from the tire. And then there was a hole in the storm: wet and jet-black, her muzzle appeared. It was caked with grains of salt. She chewed and a trickle of mineral fell from her lips. Red on black—the colors were enough to break the spell. I slapped the snow from my jeans and jacket and headed for home.

As fall changed to winter, all manner of animals took notice. The cattle grazed more intensely, tearing off great mouthfuls of sun-dried grass to stoke their boilers against the rising cold. Elk began to trickle out of the mountains. As more of them quit the high country each day in search of relative warmth and easy pickings, they began massing into larger herds. Moving across the foothills like a tide, they trailed down to the open country at night and back to the safety of the peaks with daylight.

The wolves followed close on their heels. After weeks of silence, our telemetry unit clicked to life again. Jeremy and I listened as the pack found its way back over the mountains, across the face of the Pyramid, and into Squaw Creek.

We both anticipated trouble. Even before the wolves started moving north onto the Flats, Jeremy began to send me out among the herds more often. Carrying a rifle and the radio receiver, I spent most of my waking hours with the cattle.

In spite of our preparations, the bloody day came as a surprise. I rolled out early in the morning, zipped north to check the herd, and found fifty yearlings bunched up tight beside Wolf Creek. A few hundred yards beyond them, two ruined heifers tottered through the grass and sage.

The wounds were familiar—big gashes down the hindquarters, missing bags that yawned open and shut with every painful step, flayed tails, and a pulpy mess of blood and cow shit where the rectum was supposed to be. I raised Jeremy on the radio and started the wounded heifers back in the direction of the corrals at Moose Creek.

It was a long, awful march. I tried to stay calm and take things slowly, but the heifers would have none of it. After a night of terror, they wanted only to stay with the herd. We moved in fits and starts across the land. Every hundred yards or so the heifers would turn, drop their heads, and try to rush past me. I headed them off with the four-wheeler, sometimes getting sprayed with little drops of blood as they dodged away.

At the foot of the Stock Creek bench, things went from bad to worse. In a few spots, the grade increased until I had to walk alongside the four-wheeler. The heifers were exhausted, and at times I had to nudge them along with my front bumper. Up close, their wounds looked much more extensive. The holes and scrapes were nearly symmetrical, giving the scene in front of me the aspect of a macabre optical illusion. Staring across the handlebars, I saw two identical ragged holes, each drizzling a slow stream of blood. Where flesh showed, it gleamed surreally red.

Comparing the heifers, I could see only that one was missing her asshole altogether, while the other's parts had just been sliced and torn to pieces. This, I knew, made all the difference between life and death. Holes could be stitched up. Big gashes could heal. The tail end of the digestive system, however, was irreplaceable.

For all their similarities, the heifers were marked for divergent paths. They plodded along, one potentially salvageable and the other doomed, and I followed on the four-wheeler. When the worse-off animal stopped, spread her hooves, and drizzled urine across her ruined flesh, I stepped off my machine, doubled over, and shook with dry heaves.

Both heifers moved under the weight of obvious and constant pain. When we reached the top of the bench, I did not want to push them on. It was only Jeremy's arrival in his truck, and his insistence that the heifers wouldn't be safe until we reached the small pasture adjacent to our barn and shop at Moose Creek, that kept me going.

We eased them onward, step by horrible step. Toward the end, when we were within a couple hundred yards of our destination, one of the heifers turned to fight. She ran at me, but I gunned the engine and scooted out of the way. After a few more charges, she tired and stood facing us. When Jeremy drove up close to move her on, she dropped her head and pushed in desperation against his front bumper. He honked, revved the engine, and shoved her out of the way, to no avail.

The heifer refused to walk. She stood unsteadily for a moment, then crumpled in the grass and stayed there. Jeremy thought it over, then got out and grabbed a nylon tow strap from one of the toolboxes on the truck bed. He made a loop from one end, walked up to the heifer, and snugged it down around her front hooves. I hooked the free end to his trailer hitch, and he skidded her across Badluck Way. The other heifer followed us nervously through the gate, and we left them there together.

Later in the day, while Jeremy reported the depredations to Fish, Wildlife & Parks and called Orville for a tongue-lashing and some guidance on what to do with the injured stock, I hauled water and a little grain to the heifers. They remained as we had left them—one standing and one on the ground. Hoping for the best, I set the water and feed within reach of the prone one, who lay with her head up and eyes wide.

Wake, hunt, work, hunt, sleep in a truck bed with wind screaming all around and a dog for warmth: it amounted to a hard, unforgiving rhythm. I ate meals quickly, hardly tasting them, and grew intimately familiar with the look of sunrise spreading across the expanse of the Flats.

The wolves were always there. Our radio receiver picked them up frequently, and faraway howling often served as the sound track to dusk. The Wedge Pack had come home for winter, but for the first week we didn't see them. I spent hours in likely places with binoculars and a scoped rifle, but the wolves always waited me out.

The only thing I killed during that time was the ruined heifer. I had been filling up her water bucket for several days when the word came through from Orville. The morning before I put her down, I hunted all the way up the bottom of Wolf Creek for wolves, carcasses, or fresh sign, but found only a pair of moose that caught sight of me and shoved their way through narrow passages in the willows until they disappeared from view.

The shaggy memory of the moose later reassured me somehow or at least distracted me enough to still my nervous hands and draw a bead, as per Jeremy's instructions, one inch behind the ear of the maimed heifer. When I pulled the trigger, a bloodred stream leaped out of the heifer's skull. It formed a graceful arc—smooth, shining, and big around as my pinkie finger—on the way to the ground.

The heifer went stiff, tipped over, and flexed into a flat, recumbent semicircle—a shape that brand inspectors call a lazy C—and began to move her hooves in slow ovals. A breath rattled out, and then she was nothing but a cooling mass on the great, warped plain of the Madison—one more casualty in a landscape of bones.

Since the heifer's carcass was so close to the barn, and we didn't want bears prowling around, I dug a massive hole with the backhoe and used the bucket to set her down inside. The morning after that was done, a storm blew in.

I was out checking fence in my work truck when the clouds slid across the horizon and slapped a low lid on the valley. Rain followed them in short order, then intermittent sleet and snow. The roads got snotty in a hurry, and soon I found myself creeping along in four-wheel drive, hoping I wouldn't have to get out and chain up. Peering across the North End, straining my eyes to see through the flurries, I caught sight of a bunch of heifers running at full tilt. From a distance they were a thin, black line crossing the vastness of the Flats. Though I could see nothing chasing them, the situation looked disturbingly familiar. I radioed Jeremy, who told me to go home and grab a bite of lunch while he took a four-wheeler out to see what all the commotion was about.

Just after he left, the storm turned serious. The snow thickened into a whiteout, and a vicious wind blew out of the north. I heard nothing from Jeremy for an hour, and then the radio clicked to life.

"Drive my truck out here to Stock Creek," he shouted over the wind. "Bring the rifle and a tarp."

He said something else, but the weather garbled it beyond recognition. Shortly after that, his radio went dead.

As I headed out in the truck, the temperature kept dropping and snow fell thick enough to keep the windshield wipers straining. Winter had gone on the offensive and was taking no prisoners as it roared through the valley. When I turned from the gravel of Badluck Way, all four wheels started spinning and the truck nearly bogged down. I drove alongside the road after that, finding better traction in the high grass, bumping slowly toward the edge of the Stock Creek bench.

I drove in a cocoon. Everything looked soft and faded in the blizzard's low light. Familiar objects—braces and stock tanks— seemed strange. I rolled to a stop and got out to open a metal gate. When I touched its familiar welded tubes, the caked-on snow and deep cold in the steel seemed irreconcilable with all I'd learned in summer.

I drove on across a pasture, following a little two-track road. I was nearly to the far fence when I saw the wolf emerge at a lope from the ravine that drops to Stock Creek. He sprinted away from me on a beeline toward the mountains. Against the blowing snow he was a depthless, slate-gray shade. I spun the truck to face him, skidded to a stop, and threw open the door. The wolf never turned to look at me. As I stepped into the maelstrom and reached back into the cab for my rifle, he dissolved into the storm.

At the foot of the Stock Creek bench, I found Jeremy standing near a ruined but still breathing heifer and told him about the wolf. We decided, based on the location of my sighting and the freshness of the carnage, that the wolf had been watching from the bench as Jeremy stood with the heifer. At a distance of a couple hundred yards the wolf had waited patiently while Jeremy called me on the radio, shivered against the snow, and stooped to warm his hands against the four-wheeler's engine block. The wolf sat there biding his time and thinking lupine thoughts until I rousted him out with the truck.

Jeremy put the heifer down and we wrapped the tarp around her quickly, finishing our work before her muscles stopped twitching. When the storm lifted for a bit, he pulled a pair of binoculars from the cab of the truck and glassed the foothills above us. Nothing caught his eye.

"You can bring Chad up here in the morning," he said. "It's his deal from now on."

From the way he said it, I knew that Jeremy wasn't just talking about this particular heifer or the lone wolf I'd seen on the drive out.

We swapped vehicles, since I was better dressed for the snow. Jeremy climbed into the truck, started it up, and rolled down the window. I sat on the four-wheeler, waiting for him to speak.

He glanced at the lumpy silver shape of the tarped heifer, which looked like something dropped from space, and then stared out across the wild panorama of the mountains.

"This would all be kind of funny," he said, "if it wasn't so fucking sad."

He put the truck in gear and I followed him. In convoy, we worked our way up to the top of the bench and headed south for home.

————•◦•————

Jeremy and I rode through the cattle milling in the shipping pens. They slid away from us, graceful as a shoal of fish. Dust rose thick enough to blur their moving bodies into a mass of color as we knifed through the herd, splitting off groups of twenty or a dozen according to the preferences of the truck drivers. We would have had to shout against a tide of outraged bawling to hear each other, so we mostly worked in silence.

As we moved and loaded cattle, my mind kept wandering back to the wolves. After we had put down the last heifer, Jeremy and Roger agreed out of desperation and exhaustion that the best thing we could do was turn the situation over to the professionals at Wildlife Services. We couldn't seem to catch up with the Wedge Pack. Despite our best efforts, they maimed and killed the stock with impunity, then disappeared into the hills before daylight. If summer was a war of attrition, the wolves had won it. By late September we were wrung out, shorthanded, and ill prepared for the grazing season's final push of work: gathering the herds, moving them down to pastures along Highway 287, and readying the ranch for the relentless onslaught of winter. In the midst of that last marathon, we would have no time or energy to spend on fruit-less chases across the North End.

The call was made and Chad showed up promptly with per-mits to kill three wolves. He set traps around the heifer's carcass and caught a young female. After attaching a radio collar, he set her free.

He made a traitor of her. With the trap off her leg and the col-lar broadcasting loud and clear, the female ran back into the hills and took shelter in the bosom of the pack. Chad gave us her radio frequency and Jeremy named her Judas.

Chad would have gone after the pack immediately if a big storm hadn't blown in. Low visibility and vicious winds kept the Wildlife Services helicopter grounded, giving the wolves a final, brief respite. As the snow piled up, I went out often with the re-ceiver and listened to the Judas wolf. Judging by the signals I was able to pick up, she traveled back and forth between the Mounds and Bad Luck Canyon.

Against my wishes, I developed a deep sympathy for her. The collar marked her and others in the pack for a grisly end, and every time the receiver clicked to life, the leaden weight of re-morse settled on my shoulders. The storm would break, and when it did, Chad and his pilot would be ready. As I watched the clouds pass, I hoped like hell that her transmitter would get wet, short out, and go silent.

I was moving cattle when the day came. My herd was down by the river, far from the North End. At times, over the din of squall-ing steers, I thought I could hear a straining engine and the thud of rotor blades. I never saw the helicopter, but as I rode I imagined the way it must have dropped out of the sky, guided unerringly by the signal from the Judas wolf's collar, and set the pack running across the barren expanse of the Flats. I pictured Chad leaning out the window, taking careful aim, and dropping the wolves one by one with double-aught buckshot.

Later in the day I asked Jeremy for details, but he didn't have much to say. Chad filled all three permits. The bodies of the Judas wolf and two others were collected and flown to Bozeman. The rest of the pack vanished, so far as anyone could tell, into the wild folds of the Lee Metcalf Wilderness. That was the end of it.

———·•·———

Every so often, as I worked Billy back and forth among the cattle, I glimpsed a familiar face in the steady flow of stock. I remembered strange markings, ear tag numbers, cows that were difficult and others that were docile. Some of them I had doctored, and I recalled the thrill of roping and the rattling breaths they took before falling. In the pens, over and over, it happened this way: the animal resolved from a bovine throng, I saw it for a moment, and then it crowded through the gate and disappeared. Heifer 512, the cow we had treated so roughly in the early summer, passed me in the crush, healthy, if a bit more nervous than the rest of the stock.

It was hard to keep from feeling that a summer's work had come to nothing. After five months of careful management, countless nights of standing guard, and long days of riding and doctoring, the herd was leaving. That they left much heavier than they arrived was little consolation to me, because I knew where they were headed.

I cut bunch after bunch of cattle and stuffed them into the alley, where Skogen's men whooped, hollered, and pounded them toward the chute. The cattle thudded up the ramp and into a waiting semi. Working steadily, I loaded a year's growth of grass and five months of my life into the bellies of stock trucks. Airbrakes hissing, they pulled away from the loading ramp and headed up the hill across from the Palisades to disappear, bound for the land of corn finishing.

By late afternoon the heifers and steers were gone. Only a handful of bulls, including Moses, remained in one of the side pens. While the last truck and trailer backed in, Moses stood calmly and watched the cowboys work.

One of Skogen's boys opened the gate and stepped in with the bulls. Moses ambled past him into the alley and turned toward the chute. He must not have moved quickly enough, because somebody hit him with a hotshot cattle prod. Kicking out, he broke into a trot that took him up the ramp and out of sight. The other bulls followed. A heavy, metal door clanged shut and the truck pulled away.

After we closed down the whole works, I found Orville Skogen in the scale house, totting up weights. He was fighting mad and ready to hold forth to anyone who would listen about the damage the wolves had done to his business over the summer.

"I lost my ass on this deal, you know that?" He gave me a hard look before continuing. "It's bad enough they kill a few, but that ain't even the worst part. Look at this shit!"

Orville held up a printed spreadsheet covered with scribbled numbers and notations. He explained that the heifers had come out ninety pounds light, on average.

"Ninety times seven hundred ninety! You know what that works out to?"

He didn't wait long for me to answer.

"A shitload! Seventy thousand pounds light. The sons of bitches ran seventy thousand goddamn dollars off my bottom line."

Not knowing what else to say, I told Orville I was sorry it had worked out that way. He made a little grunting noise and turned back to his figures. Remembering why I'd come, I asked him where the bulls were headed. "Some feedlot," he said. "Can't remember which one."

I told him that one of his bulls, tag R-125, was an exceptional creature. I sang Moses's praises as a gentle animal and a prolific breeder. Skogen nodded and shot me a curious, sidelong look.

"He's the kind of bull you want to keep," I said, and left him to his figures. It was the best I could do.

———·•·———

We finished shipping on the nineteenth of October. Four days later, madness descended on the lower reaches of the valley. The elk came first, spilling down from the Madisons as if a floodgate had broken open. On the ranch they congregated in the thousands, darkening hillsides and annihilating fence lines. At night they moved fearlessly around my log house, talking in strange, whistling squeals. Hunting season had begun.

Mostly I kept people off the place, but one Saturday a week or so into the season, I rose early, dressed in layer upon layer of wool without showering, and walked out to start the pickup warming. The eastern sky glowed green, and for so long as I could stand the cold, I watched it, savoring the early calm. This morning was different: I was going on a guided hunt.

I was neither the official guide nor the hunter. The clients, almost all of them from out of state, had paid handsomely to hunt bull elk on the Sun Ranch and expected their money's worth in horns. I met up with Curtis, the guide, on the main road, and he introduced me to the hunter, a young, pudgy man out from Atlanta with his father. I piled into the backseat of Curtis's truck, and as we drove up Badluck Way toward higher country, the hunter turned to me: "I want to apologize in advance—my hips are no good."

We growled uphill with the headlights off. At the road's end we slipped from the truck and gently shut the doors. The hunter loaded his rifle clumsily, and the three of us hiked uphill and climbed into the defunct ditch that used to gather water from Wolf, Stock, and Bad Luck Creeks. The ditch was about six feet deep in most places and contoured across the north half of the ranch, marking the boundary between the Flats and the crenulated foothills. The elk crossed it each morning on the way back to the mountains after their lowland night grazing.

Curtis and I crept along, peeking up occasionally to glass in the half light. We saw a handful of cows and spike bulls, but nothing worthy and nothing close. The hunter lagged behind, puffing, staggering, and tripping often over the cantaloupe cobbles in the bottom of the ditch. More than once he fell and whacked his rifle on the stones. His exertions were the loudest thing in the clear silence of the morning. The light grew and color filtered back into the world as we labored along the ditch.

We got him an elk. Well after dawn and far from the truck, Curtis spotted a legal set of antlers. We waited prone and hidden at the crest of a rise until the hunter wheezed up and cooled down enough to be steady. At two hundred yards, under close supervision, he shot and killed an unremarkable bull. The elk shuddered as the bullet hit, loped a few steps, and keeled over. We walked to where he lay. I snapped the obligatory man-with-trophy photo, and then Curtis and I gutted out while the hunter watched. He never bloodied his hands. I wondered about the story he'd tell back home.

———•◦•———

When it was my turn to hunt elk, I left the big herd on the Flats alone and chose instead to prowl the complex terrain of the South End. There was a little, run-down cabin up there, tucked in at the base of a mountain between the forks of Squaw Creek. That cabin was miles away from anything else, and I used it as a base of operations. I hiked in, set up camp, and then woke each morning before five to walk along the tributaries of Squaw and Moose Creeks. It was early in the season, before the snow piled up in earnest. I glimpsed bunches of elk through my binoculars, but they were always high on steep faces, and climbing higher. Three days passed and I never took a shot.

On the fourth day, I ranged higher and farther than before. A black bear spooked in front of me and ran like gangbusters through the trees, leaving a trail of funny, padded tracks in the mud and wet snow, which I followed for a while. After noon a group of bulls loped through my crosshairs, but I didn't like the shot. The sun was licking the horizon when I made it back to the cabin. By the time I decided to walk out to Highway 287, get my truck, and hunt farther north, it was altogether gone from the sky.

Three miles of ridges, creeks, and forest separated the cabin from the trailhead where my truck waited. The shortest route meant bushwhacking across a steep, forested drainage until I hit the overgrown road that cut through the boggy morass of the

South Fork. After that I had to skirt the edge of a huge, timbered hill and follow a faint, broken trail for half a mile. It was a piece-meal route, a path that made sense only if you knew the country.

I ate jerky and peanuts and left the cabin in an advanced state of exhaustion with only my rifle and a flashlight—anything else would have been too heavy. As soon as the cabin dropped from sight, I felt the same old fear building and blooming like a weird, pestilent flower. I was a warm, bright speck in the face of endless cold. The wild could swallow me and scatter my remains.

In this state of mind, I found myself at the end of the open sage-brush country, staring at the spot where the road cut into the trees of Squaw Creek. The close-set pines arched together above the ruts, so that the hole in the forest was as circular as a den mouth. A quarter moon dived in and out of clouds, dousing the sage with white light.

The moon winked out when I stepped between the first trees, leaving the night as black as pitch. I followed the ruts by feel more than anything, and the forest seemed to reach out at me from ei-ther side. It was like dying from the outside in: my hands and feet went cold, the blood in them stilled, and numbness crept up my arms like anesthesia.

I should have known that some things once done must be revis-ited and that, in spite of my direction and intentions, enough walk-ing would bring me back to that ovoid granite stone, that tree, and that remembered pool of shadow where we had left the big wolf. I blundered around the corner and found the white boulder sitting there with the pine's branches spread above it, unchanged.

My feet quit moving. I glanced at the stone and then twisted around to stare into the dark behind me. My senses were dull as a rusted shovel and my limbs would not answer. The rifle was dead weight on my shoulder, good for nothing. Weak-kneed and sweating in the dark, I stood paralyzed, thinking that this must be how an elk feels when the running is done, when her last reserves are gone, the blood is clumping in the dirt, and the pack is all around.

I stepped off the road, stooped into the shadow, and pressed my palm against the rough surface of the stone.

Something roared to life at that touch, like a derelict engine kicking over or embers doused with gasoline. It was as though a call came out of the dark and some part of me managed to answer.

Afterward, I went back to the road and stood for a while, listening to my heartbeat. I started walking again slowly, stopping often for small night noises and to savor the feeling of blood returning to my fingers. A half mile brought me to the edge of the forest, and I lingered in the shadows of the last trees.

At the edge of a grassy park, I looked downhill at the draw that would take me to the highway. I was loath to leave, even though I was exhausted and alone, so I loitered, prowling along the edge of the forest, toying with the idea of trying to shoot an elk at night. I sat on a little knoll and waited for something to happen. When nothing did, I walked out in the moonlight, drawn forward by hunger and possessed of strength I did not understand.

Drifts

*L*ike Dante's *Inferno,* winter on the edge of Yellowstone has levels. After hunting season ended and November fizzled out, the longest season began. Winter came as a series of shocks, each colder than the last. The weather followed a disconcerting pattern: Every few days, a storm blew in and the temperature dropped farther than I'd ever known it to do. I struggled to come to grips with each new nadir, learning the feel of ten, five, and zero Fahrenheit against the bare skin of my cheeks. After each storm, I expected some sort of break from the weather, but none came. The mercury kept falling as though it had found a new equilibrium below zero. As soon as I'd decided that I could endure a new low and got used to a set of adverse conditions, the bottom dropped out again: the thermometer fell another few degrees or the wind picked up by ten miles per hour. Overall, December felt like descending a long staircase into a deep freeze. Daylight faded further, the cold got stronger. By the middle of January, I wondered how anything left outdoors could hope to make it through to spring.

In those days I had ample time to think. Jeremy had left on a well-earned vacation, and I stayed behind as the sole caretaker of the ranch, spending my workdays in a struggle with the elements. Pipes froze. Pilot lights went out. A storm blew over power poles, plunging the Big House into frigid darkness.

For the most part, my work ended when the daylight gave out. I spent long evenings reading voraciously and watching Tick clean the ice sores between his pads. Sometimes, when the night was still, the unearthly whistling of elk came through my walls. I'd creep to the window and see shadows moving through the yard. The noise came from both sides of the house, so I'd walk from room to room, listening. A cow chirped through the kitchen window and a calf answered from somewhere beyond the couch.

On such nights I thought often of the wolves and could not blame them for the wrecks of summer. We had brought the cattle to them, after all. We bred animals for meat and docility and then dropped them on the doorstep of the howling wild. As we did it, we talked about shoehorning livestock into the ecological niches of wild grazers, the cattle functioning as part of the ecosystem. I decided that we had been a bit too successful. We had moved our stock across the land like so many buffalo or elk, and the wolves had taken notice. After a little while they'd begun to act naturally.

Neither could I fault the ranch crew much for all the rage, blood, and bullets. Like the Wedge Pack, we did our best to make a living from a hard place. Like them we came to the Madison Valley and staked our claim to the land.

I lost a lot of sleep over the wolf I'd killed, worrying endlessly over whether my actions were right, just, or ethical. I never came to a lasting conclusion. It seemed more germane and natural to say that the killing was necessary, unavoidable, and unfortunate, and then move on.

The word *coexistence* cropped up everywhere when talking about livestock and wolves. It was in my job description and on everyone's lips when we told stories about the summer's carnage. We tried like hell to coexist with the Wedge Pack, and we'd succeeded, though not in the way most people might imagine.

Our relationship with the wolves was bloody, ugly, and tortured at times, but it had worked. Over the course of the summer, the wolves killed less than 1 percent of our cattle. Despite Orville's grousing about weight, the yearlings probably made him a decent profit when they went to the stockyards. The Wedge Pack, for its part, suffered hard losses but lived to hunt another season. When all the accounts were totted up and the bones picked clean and scattered, our efforts at living with the wolves had borne real, if bitter, fruit.

———

On January 30, in the morning, the weather beat hard against the windows of the Wolf Shack and shoved down the chimney, kicking ashes across the floor. The house itself creaked like a wooden ship in swells. I waited out the worst of it. At noon the storm abated as quickly as it had come, and I went outside.

I plowed snow. Drifts abounded, thick and deceptively substantial. I got the truck stuck twice. The first time, I tried to push through too much of a bank up at the Big House and got mired to the axles. I dug around the wheels for a while, until the truck bucked free.

The second time, I slid off the road while pushing a big pile. I felt the tires spin and the truck lurch sickeningly off level but did not cut the gas as quickly as I should have. Instead I gunned the engine, tried to bull through, and ended up in the ditch with all four wheels spinning and snow halfway to the low-side windows.

Outside there was a frostbite wind that made it hard to stay calm while shoveling. I sweated from the work, but still had to hunker for shelter behind the cab. The wind blew steadily, knifing through my layers. It gathered loose ice crystals from the road and nudged steady streams of them into my diggings. It poured in with each breath and stole heat enough to remind me that lives end here, and winter takes them.

I fought off the shakes and went on working. Finally I found the frozen ground and chained up with numb fingers. When the truck broke loose in four low, it was like coming up from underwater.

At night the wind abated and left a half-moon in a cloudless sky, shining down on drifts of snow.

———•◆•———

For all my plowing and driving on snow-choked roads, I never once had to be pulled out. I'm as proud of that as almost anything. I got stuck, sometimes for hours, but never so badly that I had to call Jeremy on the radio. When I felt close to giving in, I stepped out into the cold, unhooked the shovel from the headache rack, and dug until I could see dirt around my tires. Most people weren't so lucky, careful, or stubborn.

Roger slid off Badluck Way once. He called me on the radio and I arrived to find his Subaru leaning into the borrow ditch at a wonky angle, its back axle resting on the ground. Not long after that, a visitor jammed his Jeep into a snowdrift, panicked, and spun his wheels until they dug in deep. Somebody got stuck every few weeks, but most of the time it was easy to get the vehicle back on the road. I kept a tow strap in the pickup truck, along with two sets of heavy-duty, cleated tire chains. With the chains on tight and the truck in low gear, it took only a couple of solid tugs to fix most problems.

The only real wreck we had was when Roger's son came for a visit. He brought a friend along and borrowed a truck to show him the ranch. They followed Wolf Creek upstream past the spot where it pops out of the mountains, tried to cross an icy drift, and slid down into the creek.

The kids flew back to California in the morning, but Jeremy and I worked all day with the plow truck and backhoe to save that pickup. Our final solution involved two hundred yards of heavy-duty cable, a pulley attached to the trunk of a thick tree, a high-stakes heavy-equipment balancing act, and at least a couple of moments when I doubted we would both survive the day.

Afterward, we drove out of the high country, gassed up the truck, and headed to West Yellowstone through an awful snowstorm. The flakes were so thick in the headlights that the yellow line flicked in and out of view. In other circumstances it would have seemed like pretty nervy driving. In the rescued pickup, which we had taken as a sort of trophy, the weather was just another reminder of our success and competence.

We ate pizza and drank beer in West Yellowstone, and Jeremy picked up the tab on the company credit card. He called it overtime, but the meal felt more like tribute paid from the people who owned the land on paper to those who bought it daily with measures of sweat and skill.

Moving On

*I*n March, consultants began to arrive for meetings with Roger at the Big House. The enthusiastic foreman from the summer survey crew returned to talk about "eco-communities" and present his findings in a neat show involving an easel, transparencies, and a dozen overlays. He showed maps of "Wildlife Habitat," "Migration Corridors," "Pastures," and "Easements." The last one was titled "Potential Homesites." From there it was a short step to glossy brochures featuring the ranch brand and full-color photos of the mountains.

One early-spring morning, I hiked the overgrown logging road that ran up Squaw Creek. At an old clear-cut, I looked uphill and saw the dark dirt of fresh diggings. Bear? Wolf den? I climbed the slope. A bright ribbon on a survey stake caught my eye. I walked up the Squaw Creek drainage, following a set of backhoe tracks from one test pit to another.

I could have stayed. James was still in school and Jeremy had left in March to run one of Ted Turner's bison ranches. During my final month on the place, I was alone, and worked to clear the last of winter from the roads. Every Tuesday I met with Roger, the lodge staff, a rotating cast of consultants, and a newly hired chief financial officer.

I daydreamed through most of those weekly meetings. As Roger and his managers discussed the lodge's balance sheet or hashed out a plan for advertising the lots on Squaw Creek, which was soon to be renamed Sun Creek, I looked through the window at the still-frozen wilderness outside. I remembered the way that, during a winter storm, stepping from the sagebrush flats into the forest on some north-facing slope or saddle felt as if I were dunking my head through the surface of a lake. The wind stopped. Everything went quiet. The air pressed cold and thick against my face. Snowflakes corkscrewed downward in the spaces between trees. They went slow, like bubbles in reverse.

Toward the end of each meeting, Roger always asked me for a

report on the state of the ranch. Because it was winter, and most of my time was spent keeping the machinery running and the houses warm, I often had a hard time coming up with an answer that sounded interesting enough.

"Plowed some snow," I'd say. "I paid the bills and checked fences."

Before he'd left, Jeremy teased me about stealing his job. He made some business cards on his laptop that read, "Bryce Andrews, Interim Manager, Sun Ranch," and had a graphic of our rising-sun brand in one corner. I liked those cards too well to give them away.

It wasn't loneliness that ultimately drove me off the Sun, though I sometimes got lonely. It wasn't the fact that my friends were gone. I left the ranch because I could feel something changing completely and irreversibly, like summer becoming fall.

Roger didn't carve the ranch into twenty-acre chunks, and I don't think he ever would have done that. Development would be limited to a dozen or so high-end homesites, each one worth five million dollars and sited so as to do the least possible amount of ecological damage. As far as subdivisions go, it was benign. It was a compromise, Roger said, that would keep the land pristine and allow the ranching operation to go on, while providing revenue enough to keep him from losing the place.

I could see what he was aiming for, but the devil was in the details. And having worked the ranch, I could imagine the details as well as anyone. With the homesites would come new, wider roads. Yard lights would fleck the night like cancers on a brain scan. Domestics would come and go, and in winter the home owners would slide into ditches and need rescuing. Eventually one of them would call to complain about cattle shitting on his driveway, eating his plantings, or ruining his view of the mountains.

He would call, and we would have to listen. That's what people expect for five million dollars, plus a hundred grand a year in home owners association and maintenance fees. We would change our grazing rotation, leaving the cattle longer in some other pasture to keep them away from the new houses.

The interests of cows, wolves, and elk would collide with the desires of millionaires. When they did, our stewardship of the land would suffer. I felt my job, life, and purpose on the ranch sliding into obsolescence. And so I decided to leave.

When Roger knocked on my door in mid-April, I thought he had come to wish me well. The thirtieth was my last workday on the ranch, and the Wolf Shack was in the state of thorough disarray that always precedes a move. But Roger didn't mention the fact that I was leaving, or even seem to notice all the boxes and bags strewn around. He stepped into the living room and, breathless with excitement, told me that he had seen a light-gray wolf in the vicinity of an old den at Stock Creek.

"I want you to go up there," he told me, "and see if it looks like they're using it."

I knew the spot well. In contrast to most of the places the wolves favored on the Sun Ranch, the Stock Creek den was easy to find and simple enough to monitor with a pair of binoculars from the shelter of the Mounds. It was an old hole—one that dated back to the days of the Taylor Peak Pack in the early 2000s, and had been used sporadically ever since. Because the den site was so exposed,

and Stock Creek had served as t'
oxysm of violence, I doubted ɩ.
to spend much time there.

Still, I told Roger that I'd take a ɩ
Mounds with binoculars, waiting for ɩ
across the dogtooth peaks of the Madiso.
temperature held below freezing, I could fee.
around. Light trickled back into the world, reve
that two weeks of warm afternoons had gained a
Drifts of snow lingered on steep north slopes and be.
bigger sagebrush, but most of the grasslands were meltea

As soon as I could see well enough, I trained my binoculɩ
the little grove of trees that held the den. Fresh, dark dirt spiɩ
downhill from its mouth, but that proved nothing on its own. Coyotes, badgers, and skunks sometimes lay claim to old holes. Bears
happen by and get curious. As I sat waiting for a wolf to emerge, I
turned away from the den and began to study the land around it.

I stared south across a landscape I knew by heart. From the
lofty perspective of the Mounds, I followed the familiar lines of
pasture fences as they angled across the topography of the ranch.
Looking west along Stock Creek, I recognized the spot where
Jeremy had put down the last heifer. A few scattered bones still
marked the flat where we had left her. Farther out, my gaze lingered on gates I had fixed and places where cattle moves had gone
well or haywire. I looked one last time at the dark, gaping mouth
of Bad Luck Canyon and recalled the hours I'd spent mucking out
the spring box in its shadow.

Given time, some simple tools, and a reasonable supply of re-
solve, a ranch hand is capable of scrawling his name across the

ide variety of ways. My own relics would long outlast
nce on the Sun. Twenty years from now a visitor, walk-
g any fence, but especially one running across a hilltop
elk like to hang, might find my particular brand of wire
. Perhaps she would go walking with a ranch map and find
tle spring or a hollow named for me, or something notable
id.

Man marks landscape. He does it quickly, ubiquitously, and
to such an extent in some places that it becomes impossible to
tell what was there before he started. But a place also marks a
man. I was born a Seattle boy, a water child who looked at the
clouds through holes in the trees and at the sun through holes in
the clouds. Seattle has an easy climate, provided you can stand the
rain. The land is fertile. When I spat apple seeds on the ground
and walked away, I expected trees to grow.

Not so in the Madison Valley. Seattle tends toward soft, damp
claustrophobia, but the Sun Ranch was characterized by exposure.
A wide-skied place where everything but the hard essentials dried
up and blew away, the valley and the ranch's two predominant
qualities were beauty and brutality.

That dual nature was in the weather: all summer I watched
thunderstorms roil along the horizon, blackening the sky like
bruises. One day a lightning bolt licked down and roasted a steer
in his tracks. Duality was in the animals, too: there was nothing as
eerily eloquent as the Wedge Pack's howling and nothing messier
than a kill.

Waiting in the Mounds for the emergence or arrival of wolves,
I thought back to days and nights hunting them: the thrill of chasing big, dangerous creatures through close-set timber, the pin-

226

prick stars that kept me company at night, and the guilt I lived with after finally pulling the trigger.

I shuddered to remember some of the work I did on the Sun. I had killed: an elk, a deer, a wolf-maimed heifer, and the wolf that probably tore her up. Through the long, dark months of winter those actions returned to keep me up at night. Often, I was tempted to construe ranching as nothing more than a protracted act of violence.

I thought hard about that until the sun rose high enough to light the faraway timber of the Gravelly Range. The temperature increased and a handful of deer popped in and out of sight as they negotiated the close-set hills of the Mounds. I took another look at the den's mouth, but found no motion there.

Daylight began to warm the world, melting bits of snow on the sleeves of my coat. I watched jagged little crystals of ice subside into droplets, one after another, as the sun climbed my arm. As the drops soaked my jacket's canvas shell, they seemed to argue that on a place like the Sun, things were always moving forward. Cattle got eaten. Wolves met bloody ends. Ranch hands arrived, sweated, and tried to stand against the wilderness long enough to make a living. Owners came and went, leaving their legacy in the form of strange structures and a mixed bag of place-names.

There was an element of tragedy in it, of course, but the main thing was that the land kept on. Day followed wild day, and over time amounted to a process of seasonal change. Immersion in that constant cycling was the ranch hand's highest privilege. The thought of summer coming on, the whole drama starting over with green grass, spotted fawns, and high expectations, made it hard to think of leaving.

I waited in the Mounds for another hour. When the wolves didn't show and the sun pulled away from the highest pinnacles, I gathered my things and walked to the base of the little pine grove that held the den. The wet dirt and old snow down there held a few tracks, but the process of freeze and thaw had reduced them all to ambiguous blotches.

I squatted in front of the den and peered inside. The dark oval of the mouth exhaled the thick smell of freshly turned earth. A few feet down the tunnel, pinched between the splintered fibers of a chewed-off root, a small tuft of pale fur caught my eye. I stuck my arm in after it. I couldn't reach it, so I lay down on the ground and wriggled into the hole. The bulk of my shoulders blocked the light completely, so I had to feel blindly around in search of my prize.

I nearly had my hand on it when I heard the first sound. From somewhere deeper in the hillside came a scratching noise, and then the dull thud of something readjusting its position. Though the noise didn't seem aggressive, it was enough to make a strong impression on a man wedged face-first into a hole. With my heart beating in my throat, I scooted backward toward daylight and safety, pulled free of the den, and was about to flee when the second sound reached me. Though at first I couldn't believe it, I heard the pups mewling from the underground dark.

I crouched by the den's mouth and listened for all I was worth. Here was the next generation of culprits. In a year they would be grown and hungry. They would maim and vanish, robbing some-one like me of sleep, leisure, and sanity. I might have hated them for that. Some guys I know would have fetched diesel fuel, poured it down the hole, and struck a match. But there in the pines, all I felt was a deep sympathy and curiosity. I wondered how many pups were down below, what they looked like, whether their eyes had opened, and how their lives would go. I listened to their muffled noises for a while. When I stood to leave, the sound rose above the wind—fragile, but something like a howl.

Epilogue

I left the Sun Ranch in May 2007, but could not turn away from the vastness of southwest Montana. It was impossible to forget the wolf and shake my conviction that by killing him I had taken some consequential measure of wildness from the world. I moved to Missoula, slogged through graduate school, and wrote magazine articles to pay the rent.

James, having earned his degree in Range Science from Utah State, returned in June to manage the Sun. He faced a bloody summer with an inexperienced crew: in July, the wolves began to prey on Orville's yearlings. James and his hired men struck back quickly, shooting a member of the pack, but the wolves would not be deterred. They harassed the cattle, killing what they could.

From a cramped Missoula garret, I imagined the sleeplessness, exhaustion, and mounting stress that must have prevailed on the ranch. I kept in touch with James enough to know that things went badly toward the end of July. A second wolf was killed in a manner grisly enough to make the local papers and smudge the Sun's reputation as a conservation-minded operation. In the end, Montana Fish, Wildlife & Parks elected to take out the entire pack. By December 2007, the mountains immediately above the Sun were silent and ostensibly wolfless.

I returned to the Lee Metcalf Wilderness when I could as a hunter and backpacker. Early in the summer of 2008, I hiked in and set up camp on the public land behind the Squaw Creek hogback. The high, rough country looked just as it had when I worked on the Sun. Each morning, small bunches of elk crossed the hogback, circled wide around my tent, and disappeared in the direction of the mountains. From my high perch in the foothills, the ranch's cattle could be seen grazing on the Flats below.

I walked all over, visiting Finger Lake and following the North Fork of Squaw Creek uphill until it dwindled to a trickle. A storm blew in one evening and soaked the landscape with a hard, brief shower. In the morning I packed my things and walked out, detouring on a trail that swung wide around the South Fork bog and dropped down toward Papoose Creek. In a low spot where the rain had pooled, I found a single wolf track, as big as my fist, pressed into the mud.

The Sun Ranch refused to slack its grip on my head and heart, so I kept track of it, returning in the fall of 2008 to find that the road up Squaw Creek had been improved. Though I feared I would one day find that remote drainage filled with freshly built mansions and luxury cars, development never came. The bottom dropped out of the real estate market, vaporizing the assets of would-be buyers. It hit Roger hard, too, and he sold the place in 2010 to a handful of executives from a multinational mining corporation. James lost his job when the sale went through, and moved on to run a ranch outside of Meeteetse, Wyoming. By the time Roger signed over the deed, 97 percent of the ranch's acreage was protected from development by perpetual conservation easements.

After earning a master's degree in Environmental Studies, I headed back to the mountains. I managed a different place from the Sun, the Dry Cottonwood Creek Ranch, near the has-been town of Galen in the Deer Lodge valley. There I tried to rehabilitate three thousand acres of land damaged by overgrazing and the toxic by-products of copper smelting. Though Dry Cottonwood is interesting in its own right, I am still haunted by the endless grassy sweep of the Madison Valley, the herds of elk that move like clouds across it, and the wolves running creek bottoms in the morning half light.

Acknowledgments

*I*n writing, as in ranching, no significant work gets done alone. Making a book is not so different from pushing a dead truck up a long and steepening hill. At first, when the ground is favorable and the day is young, one straining person can keep the wheels turning. At such times, it is tempting for a writer to think of a book as something that belongs to him. But then the road begins to rise. The writer's exertions fall short and progress grinds to a stop. Unless others come to join the struggle, all is lost.

Badluck Way exists because a handful of good and generous people have thrown their weight behind it and pushed hard. Kendra McKlosky was the first to do so, followed quickly by my parents, Colleen Chartier and Richard Andrews. Each supported the effort in his or her own way: Mom and Dad responded insightfully to drafts and photos, and were willing to talk endlessly about ethics, aesthetics, and ranching. Kendra lent her acute memory and creative spark to the cause. She gave me space enough to live inside my head, sometimes for days at a stretch, and then welcomed me home when the time was right.

Phil Condon improved an early draft of the book with thoughtful and open-ended critiques. Elizabeth Wales saw promise in the resulting manuscript and did an astonishingly good job of getting it into the hands of like-minded readers. I cannot imagine finding a better advocate for *Badluck Way*. Without Elizabeth's help, I would not have found my way to my editor, Leslie Meredith. Over the past year, Leslie has worked diligently and insightfully to hone the edges of *Badluck Way*. Her comments and edits have yielded a better, sharper story than the one I brought her. Leslie and others at Atria have put their hearts into supporting this book, and I appreciate it immensely.

I am grateful to Jeremy, James, and the others who worked with me on and around the Sun Ranch, including those who do not appear by name in these pages. I never meant to leave them out, only to distill life's chaos into a story that a stranger could read and understand. To Todd, Vickie, and others: the Sun belongs as much to you as it does to me or anyone else. The work you did there was essential and worthy. Thank you for all you taught me, and for your kindness.

The above people, and all the others unmentioned, have my deep and sincere gratitude. Without their gifts and efforts I would be laboring in vain, lonesome and haunted by certain indelible memories of the ranch, the cattle, and the wolves. I would have no book, half a book, or a book that falls short of its potential. These pages are not mine but ours.

About the Author

Bryce Andrews was born and raised in Seattle, Washington. He studied at Whitman College and the University of Montana, and has managed several cattle ranches in the West. He lives in Montana. This is his first book.